Getting to the Core of Writing

Essential Lessons for Every First Grade Student

Richard Gentry, Ph.D.

Jan McNeel, M.A.Ed.

Vickie Wallace-Nesler, M.A.Ed.

SHELL EDUCATION

Publishing Credits

Dona Herweck Rice, *Editor-in-Chief*; Robin Erickson, *Production Director*;
Lee Aucoin, *Creative Director*; Timothy J. Bradley, *Illustration Manager*;
Sara Johnson, M.S.Ed., *Senior Editor*; Jodene Smith, M.A., *Editor*;
Melanie Green, M.A. Ed., *Associate Education Editor*; Tracy Edmunds, *Editor*;
Leah Quillian, *Assistant Editor*; Grace Alba, *Designer*;
Corinne Burton, *M.A.Ed., Publisher*

Standards

© 2004 Mid-continent Research for Education and Learning (McREL)
© 2007 Teachers of English to Speakers of Other Languages, Inc. (TESOL)
© 2010 National Governors Association Center for Best Practices and Council of Chief State School Officers (CCSS)

Shell Education

5301 Oceanus Drive
Huntington Beach, CA 92649-1030
http://www.shelleducation.com
ISBN 978-1-4258-0915-7
© 2012 Shell Educational Publishing, Inc.
Reprinted 2013

Table of Contents

Table of Contents (cont.)

The Importance of Writing

In recent years, many school districts and teachers referred to writing as the "Neglected R" and viewed reading as the path to literacy success. Today, as research has revealed more information about the fundamental connection between reading success and writing competency, we are realizing that the road to literacy is a two-way street (Graham and Hebert 2010). While working as literacy consultants, we encountered numerous, capable teachers struggling with the complexity of implementing rigorous writing instruction. We wrote this book to enable all teachers to implement a successful writing program with a high degree of teaching competency. The success enjoyed by many of the teachers using the materials in this book has relieved frustrations, rejuvenated careers, and rekindled enthusiasm for teaching.

This book was written to fulfill two major objectives. The first objective involves motivating teachers to value and incorporate writing instruction as an essential element of literacy development. It should help them implement best practices and simplify the planning of writing instruction. New writing standards have been applied by education leaders at every level. Ultimately, the responsibility for implementing these standards is placed on the classroom teacher. Historically, the lack of emphasis on writing instruction in teacher education programs has left teachers feeling woefully unprepared to teach primary students to write, particularly at a level which meets the expectations of the standards for writing. The burden of this responsibility and feelings of inadequacy have left both experienced and novice teachers feeling empty-handed and unprepared.

Since 2010, most states have adopted the Common Core State Standards (CCSS), which are designed to provide teachers and parents with a clear understanding of what students are expected to learn. Since the CCSS are newly adopted, many teachers have not received professional development to become familiar with the standards nor have they received resources for their instruction, particularly in the area of writing. Therefore, the second objective of this book is to assist teachers in becoming familiar with these standards for writing and provide resources to support the implementation of these standards in their classrooms. *Getting to the Core of Writing* provides lessons outlining four key areas of writing: Text Types and Purposes, Production and Distribution of Writing, Research, and Range of Writing. It offers suggestions to meet those standards in instruction during Writer's Workshop. It also addresses how speaking and listening standards are easily practiced by engaging students in an interactive lesson format.

It is no secret that students become better writers by writing every day. This book contains the foundational structure and best practices that will guide teachers as they establish a daily Writer's Workshop that includes consistent, structured instruction to engage students in the writing process. Beyond that, a flexible pacing guide is provided to aid in planning writing instruction.

It is our hope that this book provides teachers with all the tools needed to inspire and equip young writers in today's classrooms.

—Richard, Jan, and Vickie

Traits of Quality Writing

The traits of quality writing continue to gain recognition as the language of successful writers. Educators at the Northwest Regional Educational Laboratory, now Education Northwest, searched for an accurate, reliable method of measuring student writing performance. Six attributes of good writing are identified in *Seeing with New Eyes* (Spandel 2005). These characteristics are used to inform and guide writing instruction.

- **Ideas** are the heart of the message, the content of the piece, and the main theme.

- **Sentence Fluency** is the rhythm and flow of the language, the sound of word patterns, and the way in which the writing plays to the ear, not just to the eye.

- **Organization** is the internal structure, the thread of central meaning, and the logical and sometimes intriguing pattern of ideas within a piece of writing.

- **Word Choice** is the use of rich, colorful, precise language that moves and enlightens the reader.

- **Voice** is the heart and soul, the magic, and the wit, along with the feeling and conviction of the individual writer that emerge through the words.

- **Conventions** are how the writer uses mechanical correctness in the piece— spelling, paragraphing, grammar and usage, punctuation, and capitalization.

Knowing and understanding the traits of quality writing supports teachers, students, and parents in thinking about writing and understanding what makes for writing success. Even in the early grades, students can communicate and recognize the characteristics of quality writing. The works of Ruth Culham (2008) and Vicki Spandel (2008) emphasize the value and benefits of using these traits to provide a common language—"a writer's vocabulary for thinking, speaking, and working like writers" (Spandel 2008, 7)—to enrich instruction and assessment in primary classrooms.

The value and importance of using this trait language in writing instruction is well supported by research (Gentry 2006). It is particularly important when working with students in the early grades to provide instructional tools to support students' different learning styles. In *Getting to the Core of Writing*, the traits are personified through student-friendly characters. Each of the characters represent a different writing trait, and collectively they are referred to as the Traits Team (traitsteam.pdf). Students are introduced to the individual team members through the mini-lessons. The Traits Team becomes a valuable tool for a Writer's Workshop experience. A more detailed description and poster of each Traits Team member is provided in the introduction to each trait section.

The Reading and Writing Connection

For years, researchers have acknowledged the reciprocal nature of the reading and writing process. For example, researchers have reported that beginning reading and writing are intricately connected and develop hand-in-hand in five early phases (Ehri 1997; Gentry 2006). Researchers such as P. David Pearson suggest that rather than teach and assess bits and pieces of reading skills and writing skills, teachers should provide deep and broad exposure to these processes, "in their more global, not their more atomistic aspect." As Richard Gentry (2006) writes, "Early writers use knowledge about sounds, letters, syllables, words, word parts like onsets and rimes, and phonics patterns, so early writing advances reading. But we haven't taken full advantage of it. Too often early reading and writing are not connected; they are treated separately."

Getting to the Core of Writing approaches Writer's Workshop from this global perspective, honoring the links between reading and writing and connecting them to the Common Core State Standards. Taken from this approach, Writer's Workshop will be an orchestra in concert—not the screeching sounds of the orchestra tuning up in bits and pieces.

When beginning readers and writers advance from nonreaders to independent, automatic, fluid readers in kindergarten through second grade, there is evidence that reading and writing develop in tandem. This is illustrated in the *Phases of Writing* chart (pages 8–9) and is adapted from a developmental monitoring process called Tracking Five Phases of Code Breaking (Gentry 2006, 2010). Beginners in a particular phase approach word reading and word writing with similar understandings and strategies. The sub-skills and cross connections of reading, writing, and spelling

strengthen naturally as students explore and become engaged in both reading and writing processes at each successive phase. There are five phases of writing development that can be observed in students as they practice writing. At each of these phases, reading and writing brain circuitry is intricately connected, and the student's responses while writing, reading, and spelling mirror each other and fit the patterns observable in the phase. Thinking about development globally rather than taking an atomistic view of isolated skills instruction will give teachers a unified perspective for monitoring progress and targeting instruction as they work with beginning writers and readers (Gentry 2006).

Phases of Writing

	Description	Writing Sample
Phase 0	• Begins at birth • Advances with widespread age discrepancies depending upon the exposure that children receive with literacy at home or in preschool • Writing is characterized by marking, drawing, and scribbling which leads to letter-like forms • First words and easy books may be mastered through reading aloud • Repeated exposure to books eventually leads to first experiences with memory reading of words and phrases	
Phase 1	• Begins when the child writes his or her name and begins using letters • Attempts to write messages and stories using letters • Imitates the reading of easy books • Does not know that letters represent sounds and has little capacity to "sound out" when reading words • Relies on pictures, logographic memory, or guessing	A flock of butterflies
Phase 2	• Expanding knowledge of the alphabet and ability to match beginning and prominent letters to sounds • Labels drawings or writes messages with a few letter-sound matches • Begins to make the voice-to-print match through finger-point reading • Can respond as writers with more elaborate pieces with appropriate instruction • Number and sophistication of books read from memory grows in Phase 2, often reaching level C (Fountas and Pinnell) or 3 (Reading Recovery; DRA) • Begins to attend to letter-sound matches at the beginning of words and write unknown words in what looks like abbreviated spelling	Humpty Dumpty

Phases of Writing *(cont.)*

	Description	Writing Sample
Phase 3*	• Reading, writing, and spelling occur by attending to one letter for each sound and by employing growing conventionally-spelled, word recognition vocabulary • Can read many books from memory • Scores of words are recognized on sight, often enabling the child to move into mid-first grade reading levels and beyond • Child is on the cusp of being an independent reader and has new strategies for figuring out unknown words, such as using word families and analogy as in *mat, cat, sat, fat, hat, rat*	They Got a Big Gatr It is 2,000 Pans.
Phase 4*	• Writers show awareness of phonics patterns • Words are spelled in "chunks" for example, *billdings* for *buildings* • Able to read easy chapter books • Can recognize 100 or more words on sight and spell many words correctly • Transitioning into second grade reading levels • Replaces memory reading with fluid decoding ability and automatic independent reading	The robin wuntid Eggs she shride dhd shride for years. BZZZ!

adapted from *Raising Confident Readers: How to Teach Your Child to Read and Write—from Baby to Age 7* (Gentry 2010).

*For a full student writing sample, please see the Teacher Resource CD (samples.doc)

The Purpose of Assessment

Assessment plays an integral role in writing instruction. It may occur at the district or state level to measure the student's ability to meet specific standards. Many classrooms include self-assessment where students use rubrics and checklists to score and reflect on their own work. Writing assessment can also take place informally as we sit and confer with young writers, taking anecdotal notes. Maintaining student writing portfolios comprised of both spontaneous and directed writing provides assessment information of a student's writing development and performance over a specific time. No matter the type or form of assessment, it should enable you to determine students' strengths and weaknesses so you may revise your instruction to meet the needs of your writers.

> *Assessment must promote learning, not just measure it. When learners are well served, assessment becomes a learning experience that supports and improves instruction. The learners are not just the students but also the teachers, who learn something about their students.*

—Regie Routman (1999, 559)

Monitoring students' writing over time provides valuable information about their growth and development. The samples, collected periodically throughout the year into student portfolios, reflect where the Writer's Workshop journey began and the student's ongoing progress and achievement relative to the instructional goals. Portfolios, along with your anecdotal notes, not only inform parents of their child's growth but also show students the variety of concepts and skills learned during Writer's Workshop.

In addition to ongoing classroom assessment, it is valuable to conduct benchmark assessments at the beginning, middle, and end of the year. The beginning of the year benchmark provides you with a baseline of data that represents the foundational skill level of the student writer. The middle and end of the year benchmarks show areas of achievement and needs as well as identify effective instructional strategies. *Getting to the Core of Writing* refers to these benchmarks as Benchmarks 1, 2, and 3 respectively. After each benchmark, it is important to analyze the student's work using the grade-level rubric (page 256; firstgradewritingrubric.pdf) in order to identify the additional support needed for the student.

Collaborating with other teachers encourages targeted conversations about student work and helps build confidence as you become more knowledgeable in interpreting and evaluating student writing. Although *Getting to the Core of Writing* includes a Suggested Pacing Guide (pages 12–13; pacingguide.pdf) and a Year-at-a-Glance plan of instruction (yearataglance.pdf) that provide benchmark prompt suggestions, it is not a one-size-fits-all classroom writing map. Your assessments and observations provide essential information to guide instructional decisions designed to meet the needs of all your students. For additional assessment resources, including benchmark support information, a rubric, a scoring guide, a classroom grouping mat, and scored student writing samples, see Appendix B (pages 254–261).

Planning Writing Instruction

Essential in any literacy development is planning and scheduling. *Getting to the Core of Writing* supports teachers as they learn and grow as writers along with their students while at the same time implementing Writer's Workshop. Growing requires nurturing like writing requires practice. The provided plan of instruction is based on the conviction that Writer's Workshop happens each and every day throughout the school year. Mini-lessons may be retaught when necessary. Some mini-lessons may require more than one day for students to fully grasp an understanding of the writing concept. Additionally, teachers proficient in writing instruction may select individual mini-lessons and teach them in an order that meets the specific needs of their students.

When writing is shared consistently and enthusiastically, students learn, love, and choose to write. As always, instruction must also be guided by the developmental needs of the students as revealed through their daily writing. The structure provided by Writer's Workshop and the lessons in this book allow both students and teacher to recognize themselves as successful writers. Once the routines of Writer's Workshop are in place, it is much easier for the teacher to focus on a quality daily writing time. Things become so routine that teachers will find themselves feeling motivated and passionate about writing instruction instead of overwhelmed.

The pacing guide found on pages 12–13 provides a suggested sequence for when to teach the lessons in this book. It serves as a guide for consistent practice in the writing process and incorporates the traits of quality writing. It is suggested that some lessons be taught more than once throughout the year.

When this occurs, if desired, the content of the student writing pieces can be modified slightly to provide students with opportunities to practice writing **opinion-**, **informative-/explanatory-**, and **narrative-**based texts. By doing this, students get to write different genres in formats that are familiar to them. For example, in Ideas lesson 1, students can change the content about which they brainstorm to create an opinion piece on why dogs are the best pet, a narrative on their summer vacation, and an informative piece on the types of plants around the school.

Planning Writing Instruction *(cont.)*

Suggested Pacing Guide

Month	Lesson
August/September	• Managing WW Lesson 1 (page 31) • Print Concepts Lesson 1 (page 53) • **Administer Benchmark 1**: Draw a picture and write a story about your favorite activity on a warm, sunny day. • Managing WW Lesson 2 (page 35) • Managing WW Lesson 3 (page 38) • Ideas Lesson 1 (page 65) • Organization Lesson 1 (page 131) • Print Concepts Lesson 2 (page 55) • Managing WW Lesson 4 (page 41) • Print Concepts Lesson 3 (page 57) • Ideas Lesson 2 (page 67) • Managing WW Lesson 5 (page 43) • Managing WW Lesson 6 (page 46) • Sentence Fluency Lesson 1 (page 85) • Print Concepts Lesson 4 (page 61) • Word Choice Lesson 1 (page 165) • Conventions Lesson 1 (page 215) • Conventions Lesson 2 (page 218) • Organization Lesson 2 (page 134) • Ideas Lesson 3 (page 70)

Month	Lesson
October	• Review Managing WW Lessons 1–6 as needed. • Print Concepts Lesson 3 (page 57) • Managing WW Lesson 4 (page 41) • Ideas Lesson 1 (page 65) • Managing WW Lesson 7 (page 48) • Ideas Lesson 4 (page 72) • Organization Lesson 3 (page 136) • Conventions Lesson 3 (page 221) • Sentence Fluency Lesson 2 (page 88) • Sentence Fluency Lesson 3 (page 90) • Word Choice Lesson 2 (page 169) • Conventions Lesson 4 (page 226) • Organization Lesson 4 (page 138) • Ideas Lesson 3 (page 70) • Managing WW Lesson 7 (page 48) • Organization Lesson 1 (page 131) • Word Choice Lesson 1 (page 165) • Ideas Lesson 7 (page 80)

Month	Lesson
November	• Review Managing WW Lessons 1–7 as needed. • Ideas Lesson 1 (page 65) • Ideas Lesson 5 (page 74) • Conventions Lesson 1 (page 215) • Word Choice Lesson 3 (page 173) • Sentence Fluency Lesson 4 (page 93) • Word Choice Lesson 4 (page 176) • Conventions Lesson 5 (page 230) • Organization Lesson 5 (page 143) • Ideas Lesson 3 (page 70)

Month	Lesson
December	• Review Managing WW Lessons 1–7 as needed. • Ideas Lesson 1 (page 65) • Conventions Lesson 6 (page 233) • Word Choice Lesson 5 (page 182) • Ideas Lesson 6 (page 77) • Organization Lesson 4 (page 138) • Conventions Lesson 7 (page 237) • Sentence Fluency Lesson 4 (page 93) • Organization Lesson 7 (page 148) • Ideas Lesson 3 (page 70)

Planning Writing Instruction (cont.)

Suggested Pacing Guide (cont.)

Month	Lesson
January	• Review Managing WW Lessons 1–7 as needed. • Ideas Lesson 1 (page 65) • Ideas Lesson 2 (page 67) • Sentence Fluency Lesson 2 (page 88) • Conventions Lesson 4 (page 226) • Organization Lesson 4 (page 138) • Sentence Fluency Lesson 5 (page 101) • Organization Lesson 6 (page 145) • Word Choice Lesson 6 (page 184) • Conventions Lesson 8 (page 240) • Ideas Lesson 3 (page 70) • **Administer Benchmark 2**: You have learned about many animals and insects. As a first grade scientist, write a report about an animal or insect. Be sure to include facts, a title, and an illustration.

Month	Lesson
February	• Review Managing WW Lessons 1–7 as needed. • Ideas Lesson 1 (page 65) • Conventions Lesson 1 (page 215) • Sentence Fluency Lesson 6 (page 110) • Organization Lesson 6 (page 145) • Word Choice Lesson 7 (page 187) • Ideas Lesson 7 (page 80) • Organization Lesson 8 (page 150) • Conventions Lesson 9 (page 243) • Organization Lesson 9 (page 153) • Ideas Lesson 3 (page 70)

Month	Lesson
March	• Review Managing WW Lessons 1–7 as needed. • Ideas Lesson 1 (page 65) • Ideas Lesson 5 (page 74) • Sentence Fluency Lesson 7 (page 112) • Word Choice Lesson 8 (page 190) • Organization Lesson 10 (page 155) • Word Choice Lesson 2 (page 169) • Organization Lesson 5 (page 143) • Conventions Lesson 5 (page 230) • Conventions Lesson 7 (page 237) • Ideas Lesson 3 (page 70)

Month	Lesson
April	• Review Managing WW Lessons 1–7 as needed. • Ideas Lesson 1 (page 65) • Ideas Lesson 2 (page 67) • Sentence Fluency Lesson 8 (page 116) • Word Choice Lesson 9 (page 195) • Organization Lesson 11 (page 158) • Organization Lesson 12 (page 160) • Conventions Lesson 9 (page 243) • Organization Lesson 2 (page 134) • Ideas Lesson 3 (page 70)

Month	Lesson
May	• *Note:* In May, revisit mini-lessons and prepare for a writing celebration. Allow students to select a piece for publication and invite guests to a reading. • Ideas Lesson 1 (page 65) • Ideas Lesson 7 (page 80) • Sentence Fluency Lesson 8 (page 116) • Word Choice Lesson 5 (page 182) • Word Choice Lesson 6 (page 184) • Organization Lesson 4 (page 138) • Organization Lesson 5 (page 143) • Conventions Lesson 7 (page 237) • Conventions Lesson 9 (page 243) • Ideas Lesson 3 (page 70) • **Administer Benchmark 3**: Write about a special experience that you would like to share with a friend. It might be a birthday celebration, a trip to the park, a visit to grandma's house, or even getting a new pet. Remember to include a beginning, middle, and end, and tell your reader details about your experience.

Components of Writer's Workshop

Writer's Workshop entails common characteristics that are essential to developing enthusiastic and successful student writers (Graves 1994, 2003; Fletcher 2001; Calkins 1994, 2005; Ray 2001, 2004; Gentry 2000, 2004, 2010). The guidelines that follow have been time-tested by years of classroom practice and collaboration with master writing teachers. The framework of this structure includes the following: the mini-lesson, writing practice time, and sharing time.

The Mini-Lesson

The mini-lesson is 5–15 minutes in length and begins the workshop. It is an opportunity to review past learning, introduce new writing strategies through modeling, and engage students in practicing those strategies through oral rehearsal. Each mini-lesson is focused on one specific topic that both addresses the needs of writers and reflects these skills as practiced by real authors. The mini-lesson is always energetic and challenges students to participate while building their confidence as writers. Students gather in a common area and become part of a comfortable, safe environment that provides guidance and encouragement.

In the appropriate mini-lessons, introduce the Traits Team poster as a visual reminder for students of the writing traits. The Traits Team includes *Ida, Idea Creator* (page 64); *Simon, Sentence Builder* (page 84); *Owen, Organization Conductor* (page 130); *Wally, Word Choice Dectective* (page 164); *Val and Van Voice* (page 206); and *Callie, Super Conventions Checker* (page 214). These characters work as a team to show students that good writing is not built one skill at a time but with a team of strategies. The Traits Team can be displayed in the classroom and referred to often to refresh students' memories of the importance for good writing.

Writing Practice Time

During the 15–30 minute writing practice, students apply the skill, strategy, or craft taught in the mini-lesson. This part of the lesson gives students practice necessary in becoming proficient writers as they compose a message to share with a reader. Simultaneously, the teacher helps individual students or small groups of students compose through conferencing. These conferences provide teachers the opportunity to praise students for applying a strategy, followed by a short teaching point. Teachers document observations in a Conferring Notebook to be used for evaluating students' progress, planning new instruction, and meeting with parents. An important part of the writing practice time is the *Spotlight Strategy*. It calls attention to one or two students briefly each day by spotlighting their work, especially when attempting the focus skill presented in the mini-lesson.

Sharing Time

The 5–15 minutes of sharing echoes the mini-lesson across Writer's Workshop and provides an additional opportunity for student talk time. At the end of the writing practice time, students are invited to spend several minutes sharing with partners, in small groups, or individually in the Author's Chair. Teachers select students to share based on their observations during writing time. A variety of sharing methods is used to promote motivation and excitement. At the end of Writer's Workshop, homework suggestions are made to help students follow up on the mini-lesson ideas. Homework can be shared on the next workshop day.

Implementing the Lessons

Each lesson supports teachers in their writing instruction and encourages students to write like published authors. Consistent language builds a commonality between students as well as across grade levels. Talking about writers, studying other writers, and practicing the craft of writing give students the gift of being an author. While the focus of the lesson may change each day, the lesson routine remains constant. Building routines in any instruction yields smooth transitions between activities and fewer opportunities for distractions. Some mini-lessons may be taught daily while others might be explored across several days. Several mini-lessons can easily be adapted to multiple themes and various pieces of literature, including those listed in the Common Core State Standards Suggested Works. It is important to consider the specific developmental levels and needs of the students. The lesson format provides structure, support, and a framework for instruction for the busy classroom teacher.

Using consistent language during each section of Writer's Workshop is one structure that students will recognize and that will be helpful for smooth transitions. Suggested language for each section of Writer's Workshop is provided in the lessons. Each Writer's Workshop lesson includes the following sections:

- Think About Writing
- Teach
- Engage
- Apply
- Write/Conference
- Spotlight Strategy
- Share
- Homework

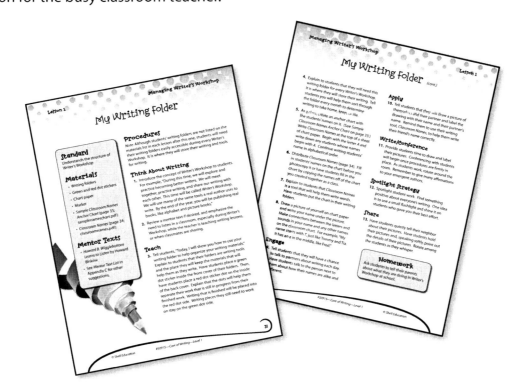

Implementing the Lessons (cont.)

Think About Writing—Students reconnect to past mini-lessons and teachers make authentic connections between reading and writing.

Procedures and **Notes**—Special information and teaching tips, followed by the explicit directions for teaching the lesson.

Standards and **Materials**—Indicates the areas of focus for the lesson and all materials needed.

Mentor Texts—Published writing that contains explicit and strong examples of the concepts addressed in the lesson. Use the recommended mentor text as a read-aloud during your reading block or quickly review it during Writer's Workshop. During writing block, focus on small samples of text that match the mini-lesson skill. Recommended mentor texts are suggested as part of each lesson. Alternative suggestions can be found in Appendix C (page 262) or on the Teacher Resource CD (mentortextlist.pdf).

Lesson 2   Managing Writer's Workshop

Looks Like, Sounds Like, Feels Like

Standard
Understands the structure of Writer's Workshop

Materials
- Chart paper
- Marker
- Sample Looks Like, Sounds Like, Feels Like Anchor Chart (page 37; lookssoundsfeels.pdf)

Mentor Texts
- Howard B. Wigglebottom Learns to Listen by Howard Binkow
- David Goes to School by David Shannon
- See Mentor Text List in Appendix C for other suggestions.

Procedures
Note: Continue building the Looks Like, Sounds Like, Feels Like anchor chart you create in this lesson each day until students reach your expectations.

Think About Writing
1. Tell students that in Writer's Workshop, writers spend time together learning how to get important ideas down on paper. To do this, we need some special rules so that we can work together as a writing community.
2. Review a mentor text if desired, and emphasize the need for order and listening in a classroom.

Teach
3. Tell students, "Today, we will think about what our writing time together should look like." Explain to students that if a visitor walked into the room during Writer's Workshop time, the visitor should see students busy drawing, writing, coloring, thinking, or talking to someone about writing.
4. Tell students they will help create an anchor chart to show what Writer's Workshop will look like, sound like, and feel like. Divide a sheet of chart paper into three columns and label the columns *Looks Like, Sounds Like,* and *Feels Like.*
5. Draw a picture of an eye at the top of the first column and list a few items to describe what the classroom should look like when someone walks into the room during Writer's Workshop. Do this as a modeled writing lesson, thinking aloud about the reasoning behind your suggestions.

Teach—Supports students through demonstration and modeling to help elevate their level of writing.

Implementing the Lessons (cont.)

Engage—Students will talk to each other about what they will apply in their writing. Talk time is short, intense, and focused. Teacher monitors, observes, and offers supportive comments.

Write/Conference—Students have essential, independent practice time. Teacher confers with students in one-on-one or small-group settings.

Spotlight Strategy—Teacher points out students' efforts and successes, emphasizing a skill or specific task to further student understanding.

Share—Students converse, explain, question, and give feedback to their groups or partners and share portions of their writing relating to the day's mini-lesson focus.

Homework—Students observe, notice, discuss, and collect important information at home and with their families that can then be used in their writings.

Apply—Students will practice what was taught in the mini-lesson, develop independence, and take ownership of their writing. Teacher restates the mini-lesson concept to solidify it for students.

Managing Writer's Workshop — Lesson 2

Looks Like, Sounds Like, Feels Like (cont.)

Engage

6. Have students turn to someone who is near them and talk about how else Writer's Workshop may look. Add any additional ideas generated from students to the anchor chart. Suggested ideas are provided on the *Sample Looks Like, Sounds Like, Feels Like Anchor Chart* (page 37); however, the majority of ideas should be student-generated.

7. Draw a picture of an ear in the next column. Talk with students about what Writer's Workshop will sound like. Repeat steps 5–6 to fill in ideas for what Writer's Workshop will sound like. You may wish to allocate one day per column in order to fully develop each concept.

8. Draw a picture of a hand in the last column. Complete the last column on the anchor chart by repeating steps 5–6 for what Writer's Workshop will feel like.

Apply

9. Tell students to draw a picture of themselves or a special friend in the class. Remind students about the *Classroom Names* chart (page 34) that is in their writing folder or displayed in the classroom. Tell students that they can use it as a tool for how to spell their friends' names. Also, they will practice what Writer's Workshop looks like, sounds like, and feels like as they are working.

Write/Conference

10. Provide time for students to draw and label their pictures. Conferencing with students will begin once procedures are firmly in place. Help any students who need assistance get settled into the writing time. Then, as students work, rotate around the room. Notice and compliment writing as students work. Remember to give many affirmations to your emergent authors.

Spotlight Strategy

11. Spotlight student work by making positive comments such as, "José is making a wonderful picture. He can save that picture and use it as an idea for a story."

12. Encourage writers to continue their writing by adding details to their pictures. Remind students that this is what our classroom should look like during Writer's Workshop time.

Share

13. Have students share their writing at their desks. Have them hold their pictures and softly tell their neighbors about the details in their pictures. Rotate among the students as they share with each other.

> **Homework**
> Ask students to tell their parents about what they are doing in Writer's Workshop time at school.

36   #50915—Core of Writing—Level 1   © Shell Education

Implementing Writer's Workshop

Writer's Workshop-at-a-Glance

This chart provides an at-a-glance overview of the Writer's Workshop format provided in *Getting to the Core of Writing*. It can be a helpful tool to use when planning instruction.

Component	Time	Description
Mini Lesson	5–15 minutes	Lesson plan subsections include: • Think About Writing • Teach • Engage • Apply
Writing Practice	15–30 minutes	Lesson plan subsections include: • Write/Conference • Praise accomplishments • Make a teaching point • Use Conferring Log • Spotlight Strategies
Sharing	5–15 minutes	Lesson plan subsections include: • Share • Whole/small group • Partners • Compliment and comment • Homework

The Writing Conference

Writing conferences are most successful when they occur as a conversation between two writers who are simply talking about writing. It is a time to value students as writers, to differentiate instruction, to teach new strategies, and to gather information for forming instructional decisions. Anderson (2000) notes that a conference conversation basically includes two parts: conversation based upon the student's current writing and conversation based on what will help him or her become a better writer. Katie Wood Ray (2001) and Lucy Calkins (2003) tell us conferring is hard! It is one part of the day that is a bit unknown. When conferring one-on-one with young writers, there is no script—no specific plan developed prior to the meeting. That is a strong deterrent that can keep many teachers from stepping into the conferring role during Writer's Workshop.

Following Calkins's dictum: "Conferring is the heart of Writer's Workshop" (2003, VIII), the sharing of information in conference conversation over the development of a specific writing piece is the very heart of teaching writing. Although difficult at times, especially at first, even the smallest conversation lets your students know you are interested in them as writers and helps nudge them forward in their writing development. Just as students become better writers by writing, you will only become better at conferring by conferring. The sincerity with which you approach this task will not only affect your students' writing future but also your sense of accomplishment as a teacher.

Although the content of the conference conversation is unknown, the conference structure is predictable. The four phases of a conference structure are:

1. Observe
2. Praise
3. Guide
4. Connect

First, study to determine what the writer knows, what the writer is trying to do, and what the writer needs to learn. Next, provide praise. Then, develop a teaching point and guide and encourage the writer to practice that teaching point. Lastly, stress the importance of using what was learned in future writing. For a more detailed explanation of each phase, see Appendix A (page 246–253).

The Writing Conference (cont.)

Included in Appendix A and on the Teacher Resource CD are additional resources dedicated to the subject of conferring with students.

- **Essential Materials**—Use this list to assemble a "toolkit" of items you can carry with you as you conference with students.

- **Mini-Lesson Log**—Keep a record of the mini-lessons taught to serve as a reminder of writing strategies and crafts students have been exposed to during whole-group instruction (minilessonlog.pdf).

- **Conference Log**—This conference form serves as a good starting point and makes it easy to view your entire class at one glance. It is a simple summary of the conference listing the name, date, praise, and teaching point. See pages 246–250 in Appendix A for more information on conferring steps. Some teachers prefer a separate conference page for each student as they become more familiar with the conferring process (conferencelog.pdf).

- **Conference Countdown**—This page lists simple reminders of salient points to consider during writing conferences (conferencecountdown.pdf).

When you take the time to have a conversation, you are sending a message that you care enough to listen and communicate. With so much emphasis on testing achievement, it is important to stay committed to teaching the writer and not just the work of the writer. Carl Anderson (2000) tells us that student efforts and achievements are most likely not due to the questions we ask, the feedback we give, or our teaching. He states, "In the end, the success of a conference often rests on the extent to which students sense we are genuinely interested in them as writers—and as individuals" (page 22).

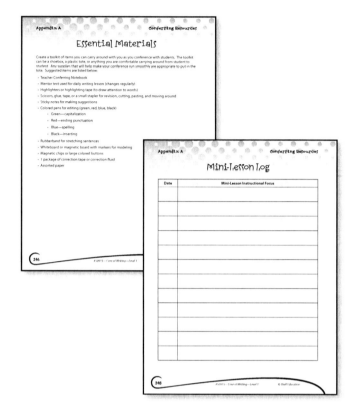

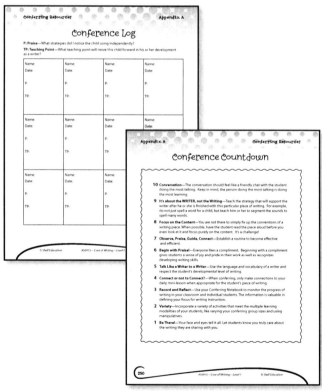

Top 10 Tips for Creating Successful Writers

1. **Schedule Writer's Workshop Daily.** Scheduling Writer's Workshop daily grants valuable, necessary time for students to practice and grow as writers.

2. **Establish and Commit to Routines.** Life is good when everyone knows what to do and when to do it. Take the time to establish foundational routines that will impact your Writer's Workshop throughout the year. Revisit Managing Writer's Workshop lessons as the need arises.

3. **Model, Model, Model!** Modeling gives direct instruction while scaffolding for young writers. Use these steps to model specific skills and behaviors with students (*I* is the teacher and *you* is the student) (Pearson and Gallager 1983):

   - I do, you watch.
   - I do, you help.
   - You do, I help.
   - You do, I watch.

4. **Read, Read, Read!** Reading a variety of texts through the eyes of a writer exposes students to the craft of the author and encourages students to explore new avenues of writing.

5. **Display and Celebrate!** Walking down the hallway in a school setting, you can usually get a good idea of the writing that is going on in each classroom. The more students write, the more comfortable they become, and they will want to show off their work. Celebrate student writing and recognize students as writers.

6. **Confer Weekly.** This is your opportunity to learn about each student's writing development. Encourage, guide, and listen.

7. **Share, Share, Share!** Young children love to share everything. Sharing during Writer's Workshop enhances their sense of importance as a writer.

8. **Involve and Inform Parents.** Writing work is an automatic means of connecting with parents. Wall displays of writing samples show parents how you value their child's writing effort. Hold an Author's Tea and invite parents so they can see first-hand the important writing work of their child.

9. **Be Flexible and Reflect.** A well-planned lesson may fall flat. So, go back to the drawing board and ask yourself, "Why?" "What happened?" How can you reteach to make the right connections for students? Take time to reflect on your teaching and student learning.

10. **Set High Expectations.** Be specific with your expectations and articulate clearly what you would like the students to accomplish. Believe in your students' abilities and challenge them to succeed. Every child can be an author.

Correlation to Standards

Shell Education is committed to producing educational materials that are research- and standards-based. In this effort, we have correlated all of our products to the academic standards of all 50 United States, the District of Columbia, the Department of Defense Dependent Schools, and all Canadian provinces. We have also correlated to the **Common Core State Standards**.

How To Find Standards Correlations

To print a customized correlation report of this product for your state, visit our website at **http://www.shelleducation.com** and follow the on-screen directions. If you require assistance in printing correlation reports, please contact Customer Service at 1-877-777-3450.

Purpose and Intent of Standards

Legislation mandates that all states adopt academic standards that identify the skills students will learn in kindergarten through grade twelve. Many states also have standards for Pre-K. This same legislation sets requirements to ensure the standards are detailed and comprehensive.

Standards are designed to focus instruction and guide adoption of curricula. Standards are statements that describe the criteria necessary for students to meet specific academic goals. They define the knowledge, skills, and content students should acquire at each level. Standards are also used to develop standardized tests to evaluate students' academic progress. Teachers are required to demonstrate how their lessons meet state standards. State standards are used in the development of all of our products, so educators can be assured they meet the academic requirements of each state.

McREL Compendium

We use the Mid-continent Research for Education and Learning (McREL) Compendium to create standards correlations. Each year, McREL analyzes state standards and revises the compendium. By following this procedure, McREL is able to produce a general compilation of national standards. Each lesson in this product is based on one or more McREL standard. The chart on the following pages and on the Teacher Resource CD (standards.pdf) lists each standard taught in this product and the page number(s) for the corresponding lesson(s).

TESOL Standards

The lessons in this book promote English language development for English language learners. The standards listed on the Teacher Resource CD (standards.pdf) support the language objectives presented throughout the lessons.

Common Core State Standards

The lessons in this book are aligned to the Common Core State Standards (CCSS). The standards on pages 25–26 and on the Teacher Resource CD (standards.pdf) support the objectives presented throughout the lessons.

Correlation to Standards (cont.)

McREL Standards

Standard	Lesson
Understands the structure of Writer's Workshop	My Writing Folder (page 31); Looks Like, Sounds Like, Feels Like (page 35); Guidelines for Writer's Workshop (page 38); Two-Inch Voices (page 41); Turn and Talk (page 43); Posture and Pencil Grip (page 46); Sharing (page 48)
Uses prewriting strategies to plan written work	Ideas Thinking Chart (page 65); My Idea Bank (page 67); Getting Ideas from Literature (page 70); Kings and Queens of Writing (page 72); My Expert List (page 74); Places I Love (page 77); People I Love (page 80)
Uses strategies to draft and revise written work	Using Sentence Stems (page 85); Popcorn Sentences (page 88); Super Sentence Stems (page 90); Building Sentences 1—Subjects (page 93); Building Sentences 2—Predicates (page 101); Building Sentences 3—Details (page 110); Crawlin' Phrases (page 112); The Sentence Game (page 116); And Then… (page 122); Writing Detectives: Sentences (page 124)
Uses strategies to edit and publish written work	The Capital Rap (page 218); Movin' to Edit (page 230); My Writing Checklist (page 237); Perfect Punctuation (page 240); My Editing Guide (page 243)
Uses strategies to organize written work	Matching Text to Picture (page 131); Making Alphabet Books (page 134); Hand Plan (page 138); Telling, Sketching, and Writing Informative Text (page 143); Telling, Sketching, and Writing Narrative Text (page 145); Using Speech Bubbles (page 148); Writing a Letter (page 150); Poetry: Simple Acrostic (page 158); Poetry: Five Ws Poem (page 160)
Uses writing and other methods to describe familiar persons, places, objects, or experiences	Using Words to Paint a Picture (page 169); More Than Big and Little (page 173); I Say It with My Senses (page 176); Amazing Words (page 187); Transition Words (page 190); Sounds All Around from A to Z (page 195)
Writes in a variety of forms or genres	Making Alphabet Books (page 134); My First Book (page 136); Telling, Sketching, and Writing Informative Text (page 143); Telling, Sketching, and Writing Narrative Text (page 145); Using Speech Bubbles (page 148); Writing a Letter (page 150); Addressing an Envelope (page 153); I Know How To… (page 155); Poetry: Simple Acrostic (page 158); Poetry: Five Ws Poem (page 160)

Correlation to Standards (cont.)

McREL Standards (cont.)

Standard	Lesson
Writes expressive compositions (uses an individual, authentic voice)	More Than Happy, Sad, and Mad (page 207); Voice Times Two (page 210)
Uses descriptive words to convey basic ideas	Using Words to Paint a Picture (page 169); More Than Big and Little (page 173); I Say It with My Senses (page 176); Awesome Adjectives (page 182); Show Me: Using Action Words (page 184); Amazing Words (page 187); Transition Words (page 190); Sounds All Around from A to Z (page 195)
Uses conventions of print in writing	Connecting Sounds to Names (page 53); Where to Start! Left to Right and Return Sweep (page 55); Directionality and Lowercase Letters (page 57); Spacing (page 61)
Uses complete sentences in written compositions	Building Sentences 1—Subjects (page 93); Building Sentences 2—Predicates (page 101); Building Sentences 3—Details (page 110); The Sentence Game (page 116); Writing Detectives: Sentences (page 124)
Uses verbs in written compositions	Show Me: Using Action Words (page 184)
Uses adjectives in written compositions	Awesome Adjectives (page 182)
Uses conventions of spelling in written compositions	Using High Frequency Words (page 165); Using the Alphabet Chart (page 215); Using the Vowel Chart (page 221); Hear It! Say It! Sound Boxes (page 226); Using the Digraphs and Blends Chart (page 233)
Uses conventions of capitalization in written compositions	The Capital Rap (page 218); Movin' to Edit (page 230)
Uses conventions of punctuation in written compositions	Movin' to Edit (page 230); Perfect Punctuation (page 240)
Makes contributions in class and group discussions	All lessons
Asks and responds to questions	All lessons
Follows rules of conversation and group discussion	All lessons
Gives and responds to oral directions	All lessons

Correlation to Standards (cont.)

Common Core State Standards

The purpose of the Common Core State Standards is to guarantee that all students are prepared for college and career literacy as they leave high school. These standards indicate that all students need the ability to write logical opinions and informational texts with sound reasoning to support their findings. *Getting to the Core of Writing* provides the fundamental writing skills to support students in their continued growth as writers, thus enabling them to enjoy continued success as the challenges presented by the curriculum become increasingly complex.

The structure of Writer's Workshop and the lessons in this book address the Common Core State Standards for **writing**. They also address **speaking and listening** standards, which are the building blocks of written language, through the Engage and Share components of the lesson. Due to the reciprocal nature of reading and writing, *Getting to the Core of Writing* naturally meets many of the Common Core State Standards for **reading** and for **language** as well. The standards below can also be found on the Teacher Resource CD (standards.pdf).

Standard	Lesson
Writing: Text Types and Purposes, W.1.1	Getting Ideas from Literature (page 70); Making Alphabet Books (page 134); My First Book (page 136); Hand Plan (page 138); Using Speech Bubbles (page 148); Writing a Letter (page 150)
Writing: Text Types and Purposes, W.1.2	Getting Ideas from Literature (page 70); Making Alphabet Books (page 134); My First Book (page 136); Hand Plan (page 138); Telling, Sketching, and Writing Informative Text (page 143); Using Speech Bubbles (page 148); Writing a Letter (page 150); I Know How To... (page 155)
Writing: Text Types and Purposes, W.1.3.	Getting Ideas from Literature (page 70); My First Book (page 136); Hand Plan (page 138); Telling, Sketching, and Writing Narrative Text (page 145); Using Speech Bubbles (page 148); Writing a Letter (page 150); Transition Words (page 190)
Writing: Production and Distribution of Writing, W.1.5	All lessons
Writing: Research to Build and Present Knowledge, W.1.7	Getting Ideas From Literature (page 70); My First Book (page 136); Hand Plan (page 138); Telling, Sketching, and Writing Informative Text (page 143); I Know How To... (page 155)
Writing: Research to Build and Present Knowledge, W.1.8	Getting Ideas From Literature (page 70); Hand Plan (page 138); I Know How To... (page 155); Telling, Sketching, and Writing Informative Text (page 143)

Correlation to Standards (cont.)

Common Core State Standards (cont.)

Standard	Lesson
Speaking and Listening: Comprehension and Collaboration, SL.1.1	All lessons
Speaking and Listening: Comprehension and Collaboration, SL.1.2	All lessons
Speaking and Listening: Comprehension and Collaboration, SL.1.3	All lessons
Speaking and Listening: Presentation of Knowledge and Ideas, SL.1.4	Looks Like, Sounds Like, Feels Like (page 35); Kings and Queens of Writing (page 72); Matching Text to Picture (page 131); Using Words to Paint a Picture (page 169); More Than Big and Little (page 173); I Say It with My Senses (page 176); Awesome Adjectives (page 182)
Speaking and Listening: Presentation of Knowledge and Ideas, SL.1.5	Ideas Thinking Chart (page 65); Kings and Queens of Writing (page 72); Matching Text to Picture (page 131); Telling, Sketching, and Writing Informative Text (page 143); Telling Sketching, and Writing Narrative Text (page 145); I Know How To... (page 155); More Than Happy, Sad, and Made (page 207)
Speaking and Listening: Presentation of Knowledge and Ideas, SL.1.6	All lessons
Language: Conventions of Standard English, L.1.1	All Sentence Fluency lessons; Awesome Adjectives (page 182); Show Me: Using Action Words (page 184); Transition Words (page 190)
Language: Conventions of Standard English, L.1.2	My Writing Folder (page 31); All Print Concepts lessons; Using High Frequency Words (page 165); All Conventions lessons
Language: Vocabulary Acquisition and Use, L.1.4.	More Than Big and Little (page 173); More Than Happy, Sad, and Mad (page 207)
Language: Vocabulary Acquisition and Use, L.1.5.	Building Sentences 3—Details (page 110); Using Words to Paint a Picture (page 169); More Than Big and Little (page 173); I Say It with My Senses (page 176); Awesome Adjectives (page 182); Show Me: Using Action Words (page 184); Amazing Words (page 187); Sounds All Around from A to Z (page 195); More Than Happy, Sad, and Mad (page 207)
Language: Vocabulary Acquisition and Use, L.1.6.	Getting Ideas from Literature (page 70); Building Sentences 3—Details (page 110); Crawlin' Phrases (page 112); The Sentence Game (page 116); Transition Words (190)

Acknowledgments

We stand on the shoulders of national and world-renowned teachers of teachers-of-writing, such as our friend the late Donald Graves, Lucy Calkins, Ralph Fletcher, Donald Murry, Vicki Spandel, Ruth Culham, Katie Wood Ray, Carl Anderson, Charles Temple, Jean Gillet, Stephanie Harvey, Debbie Miller, Regie Routman, Marissa Moss, Steve Graham, and Connie Hebert to name a few, as well as educators at Northwest Regional Educational Laboratory. Thank you. We are also truly grateful to the faculty at Auckland University, workshop leaders, and experiences with the teachers in New Zealand some 20 years ago who got us started.

While writing this series and in the past, there were frequent chats about writing and words of wisdom from Dona Rice, Sara Johnson, Jean Mann, Lois Bridges, and Tim Rasinski. Scores of teachers who read our manuscripts, praised our work, gave us confidence, and adjusted our missteps. We could not have succeeded without two super editors, Dona and Sara, and the great staff at Teacher Created Materials/ Shell Education.

We attribute much of what's good about our series to teachers who invited us into their classrooms. Over all the years that went into this project, there are too many people to list separately, but here's a sampling: Thank you to all the teachers and districts who allowed us to visit and model in your classrooms, try our materials, and listen to your insights as we refined our writing instruction. A special thank you to the teachers at Fayette, Logan, Mingo, Pocahontas, Upshur, Wood, Wirt, and Harrison County Schools. We owe special gratitude to French Creek Elementary, Mt. Hope Elementary, and Nutter Fort Elementary teachers. We can't forget the "Writing Teachers Club": Debbie Gaston, Tammy Musil, Judy McGinnis, Jenna Williams, Cheryl Bramble, Karen Vandergrift, Barb Compton, Whitney Fowler, and Jennifer Rome, who spent countless hours learning, questioning, and sharing ideas. "You really need to write a book," you said, and your words have made that happen. You and many others inspired us, including the WC Department of Teaching and Learning (especially Angle, Karen, Lesley, Marcia, Matt, M.C., and Wendy). We can't forget Jean Pearcy, Miles 744, the talented teachers of the West Clermont Schools, the 4 B's (Bailey, Bergen, Blythe, and Brynne), Candy, Mrs. Hendel, the lab rats (Becky, Mary, Mike, Sally, Sharon, and Vera), and the littlest singers at CHPC. Last but not least, a special thank you to Rick and Ro Jensen, Bill McIntyre, and Carolyn Meigs for years of support, and to Dawna Vecchio, Loria Reid, Terry Morrison, Laura Trent, Jeanie Bennett, Millie Shelton, Therese E., and Kathy Snyder for listening, cheering, and celebrating!

Many thanks to administrators who provided opportunities, leadership, and support for teachers as they explored the implementation of writing workshop and applied new teaching strategies: superintendents Beverly Kingery, Susan Collins, director Kay Devono, principals Allen Gorrell, Frank Marino, Joann Gilbert, Pattae Kinney, Jody Decker, Vickie Luchuck, Jody Johnson, and Wilma Dale. We owe many thanks to WVDE Cadre for continuous professional development—you brought us together.

We owe immense gratitude for having been blessed with the company of children who have graced us with their writing, creativity, and wisdom. Thank you to hundreds of children who have shared marvelous writing and insight.

Finally, for never-ending patience, love and support we thank our families: Clint, Luke, and Lindsay; Lanty, Jamey, John, Charlie, Jacki, Jeffrey; and Bill. You all are the best!

About the Authors

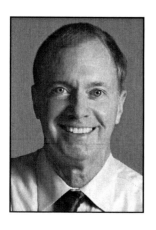

Richard Gentry, Ph.D., is nationally recognized for his work in spelling, phase theory, beginning reading and writing, and teaching literacy in elementary school. A former university professor and elementary school teacher, his most recent book is *Raising Confident Readers: How to Teach Your Child to Read and Write—From Baby to Age 7*. Other books include topics such as beginning reading and writing, assessment, and spelling. He also blogs for *Psychology Today* magazine. Richard has spoken at state and national conferences and has provided teachers with inspiring strategies to use in their classroom.

Jan McNeel, M.A.Ed., is a forty-year veteran of education and leader of staff development throughout West Virginia and Maryland. Formerly a Reading First Cadre Member for the West Virginia Department of Education and Title I classroom and Reading Recovery teacher, Jan consults with schools and districts across the state. Jan's studies of literacy acquisition at the Auckland University in New Zealand serve as the foundation of her expertise in reading and writing. Her practical strategies and useful ideas are designed to make reading and writing connections that are teacher-friendly and easy to implement. She has won awards for her excellent work as a master teacher and has presented her work in early literacy at state, regional, and national conferences.

Vickie Wallace-Nesler, M.A.Ed., has been in education for 30 years as an itinerant, Title 1, and regular classroom teacher. Through her current work as a Literacy Coach for grades K–5, conference presenter, and literacy consultant, Vickie brings true insight into the "real world" of educators and their challenges. That experience, along with Master's degrees in both Elementary Education and Reading, National Board certification in Early and Middle Literacy for Reading and Language Arts, and studies at The Teachers College Reading and Writing Project at Columbia University, drive her passion for helping all teachers and students develop a love for learning.

Managing Writer's Workshop

Writer's Workshop begins on the first day of school and is taught every day thereafter. Establishing routines is critical to developing a successful and productive writing time. Therefore, management lessons should be focused on early in the year and revisited when necessary. Managing Writer's Workshop mini-lessons require time and repetition to develop automaticity during Writer's Workshop. Repeat mini-lessons as needed, especially on the topics of guidelines for Writer's Workshop and sharing writing with partners. These two particular lessons will be crucial to having Writer's Workshop run smoothly and successfully for the rest of the year. Ensure that students are responding to those lessons in the ways you want them to or spend additional time teaching and modeling. Observe your class to find the needs of your particular students. Lessons in this section include:

- Lesson 1: My Writing Folder (page 31)
- Lesson 2: Looks Like, Sounds Like, Feels Like (page 35)
- Lesson 3: Guidelines for Writer's Workshop (page 38)
- Lesson 4: Two-Inch Voices (page 41)
- Lesson 5: Turn and Talk (page 43)
- Lesson 6: Posture and Pencil Grip (page 46)
- Lesson 7: Sharing (page 48)

My Writing Folder

Standard

Understands the structure of Writer's Workshop

Materials

- Writing folders
- Green and red dot stickers
- Chart paper
- Marker
- *Sample Classroom Names Anchor Chart* (page 33; samplenameschart.pdf)
- *Classroom Names* (page 34; classroomnames.pdf)

Mentor Texts

- *Howard B. Wigglebottom Learns to Listen* by Howard Binkow
- See *Mentor Text List* in Appendix C for other suggestions.

Procedures

Note: Although students' writing folders are not listed on the materials list in each lesson after this one, students will need their writing folders easily accessible during every Writer's Workshop. It is where they will store their writing and tools for writing.

Think About Writing

1. Introduce the concept of Writer's Workshop to students. For example, "During this time, we will explore and practice becoming better writers. We will meet together, practice writing, and share our writing with each other. This time will be called *Writer's Workshop*. We will use many of the same tools a real author uses to write. By the end of the year, you will be publishing real books, like alphabet and picture books."

2. Review a mentor text if desired, and emphasize the need to listen in a classroom, especially during Writer's Workshop, while the teacher is teaching writing lessons, or when classmates are sharing.

Teach

3. Tell students, "Today, I will show you how to use your writing folder to help organize your writing materials." Explain to students that their folders are writing tools and the place they will keep the materials that will help them as they write. Have students place a green dot sticker inside the front cover of their folders. Then, have students place a red dot sticker dot on the inside of the back cover. Explain that the dots will help them separate their work that is still in progress from their finished work. Writing that is finished will be placed into the red dot side. Writing pieces they still need to work on stay on the green dot side.

My Writing Folder (cont.)

4. Explain to students that they will need this writing folder for every Writer's Workshop. It is where they will store their writing. Tell students you will help them sort through the folder every month to determine writing to take home, keep, or file.

5. As a class, create an anchor chart with the students' names on it. (See *Sample Classroom Names Anchor Chart* on page 33.) Write *Classroom Names* at the top of a sheet of chart paper. Begin with the letter *A* and write down any students whose names begin with *A*. Continue writing students' name in alphabetical order.

6. Distribute *Classroom Names* (page 34). Fill in students' names on the chart before you photocopy it or have students fill in the chart by copying the names off of the chart you created together as a class.

7. Explain to students that *Classroom Names* is a tool that will help them write words. Have students put the chart in their writing folders.

8. Draw a picture of yourself on chart paper and write your name under the picture. Make connections between the letters and sounds in your name and any other names on the classroom chart. For example, "My name starts with *T*, just like Tommy and Tia. It has an *e* in the middle, like Fred."

Engage

9. Tell students that they will have a chance to talk to partners about writing each day. Have students talk to the person next to them about how their names are alike and different.

Apply

10. Tell students that they will draw a picture of themselves and their partner and label the drawing with their name and their partner's name. Remind them to use their writing tool, *Classroom Names*, to help them write their friend's name correctly.

Write/Conference

11. Provide students time to draw and label their pictures. Conferencing with students will begin once procedures are firmly in place. As students work, rotate around the room. Remember to give many affirmations to your emergent authors.

Spotlight Strategy

12. Spotlight student work. Find something positive about everyone's writing. One idea is to use a small flashlight and shine it on students who gave you their best effort.

Share

13. Have students quietly tell their neighbor about their pictures. Have students hold their pictures and, speaking softly, point out the details of their pictures. Rotate among the students as they whisper.

Homework

Ask students to tell their parents about what they are doing in Writer's Workshop at school.

Sample Classroom Names Anchor Chart

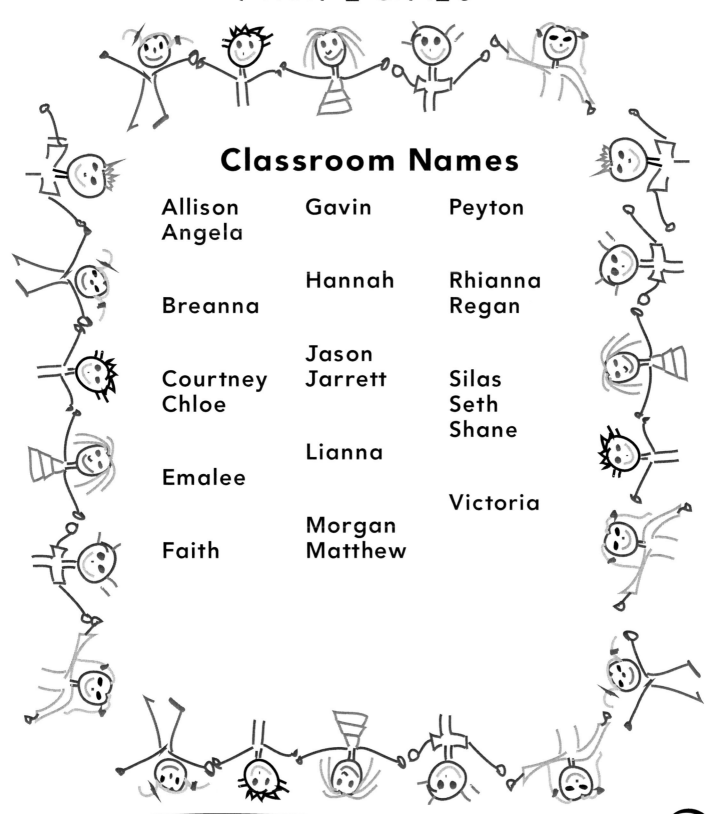

Classroom Names

Allison	Gavin	Peyton
Angela		
	Hannah	Rhianna
Breanna		Regan
	Jason	
Courtney	Jarrett	Silas
Chloe		Seth
		Shane
	Lianna	
Emalee		Victoria
	Morgan	
Faith	Matthew	

Classroom Names

Looks Like, Sounds Like, Feels Like

Standard

Understands the structure of Writer's Workshop

Materials

- Chart paper
- Marker
- *Sample Looks Like, Sounds Like, Feels Like Anchor Chart* (page 37; lookssoundsfeels.pdf)

Mentor Texts

- *Howard B. Wigglebottom Learns to Listen* by Howard Binkow
- *David Goes to School* by David Shannon
- See *Mentor Text List* in Appendix C for other suggestions.

Procedures

Note: Continue building the Looks Like, Sounds Like, Feels Like anchor chart you create in this lesson each day until students reach your expectations.

Think About Writing

1. Tell students that in Writer's Workshop, writers spend time together learning how to get important ideas down on paper. To do this, we need some special rules so that we can work together as a writing community.

2. Review a mentor text if desired, and emphasize the need for order and listening in a classroom.

Teach

3. Tell students, "Today, we will think about what our writing time together should look like." Explain to students that if a visitor walked into the room during Writer's Workshop time, the visitor should see students busy drawing, writing, coloring, thinking, or talking to someone about writing.

4. Tell students they will help create an anchor chart to show what Writer's Workshop will look like, sound like, and feel like. Divide a sheet of chart paper into three columns and label the columns *Looks Like*, *Sounds Like*, and *Feels Like*.

5. Draw a picture of an eye at the top of the first column and list a few items to describe what the classroom should look like when someone walks into the room during Writer's Workshop. Do this as a modeled writing lesson, thinking aloud about the reasoning behind your suggestions.

Looks Like, Sounds Like, Feels Like *(cont.)*

Engage

6. Have students turn to someone who is near them and talk about how else Writer's Workshop may look. Add any additional ideas generated from students to the anchor chart. Suggested ideas are provided on the *Sample Looks Like, Sounds Like, Feels Like Anchor Chart* (page 37); however, the majority of ideas should be student-generated.

7. Draw a picture of an ear in the next column. Talk with students about what Writer's Workshop will sound like. Repeat steps 5–6 to fill in ideas for what Writer's Workshop will sound like. You may wish to allocate one day per column in order to fully develop each concept.

8. Draw a picture of a hand in the last column. Complete the last column on the anchor chart by repeating steps 5–6 for what Writer's Workshop will feel like.

Apply

9. Tell students to draw a picture of themselves or a special friend in the class. Remind students about the *Classroom Names* chart (page 34) that is in their writing folder or displayed in the classroom. Tell students that they can use it as a tool for how to spell their friends' names. Also, they will practice what Writer's Workshop looks like, sounds like, and feels like as they are working.

Write/Conference

10. Provide time for students to draw and label their pictures. Conferencing with students will begin once procedures are firmly in place. Help any students who need assistance get settled into the writing time. Then, as students work, rotate around the room. Notice and compliment writing as students work. Remember to give many affirmations to your emergent authors.

Spotlight Strategy

11. Spotlight student work by making positive comments such as, "José is making a wonderful picture. He can save that picture and use it as an idea for a story."

12. Encourage writers to continue their writing by adding details to their pictures. Remind students that this is what our classroom should look like during Writer's Workshop time.

Share

13. Have students share their writing at their desks. Have them hold their pictures and softly tell their neighbors about the details in their pictures. Rotate among the students as they share with each other.

Homework

Ask students to tell their parents about what they are doing in Writer's Workshop time at school.

Sample Looks Like, Sounds Like, Feels Like Anchor Chart

Our Writer's Workshop...

Looks Like	Sounds Like	Feels Like

• Pencils, all supplies ready • Journals/folders/notebooks • Crayons/art paper • Word walls • Mentor texts available • Phonics charts/alphabet charts • Labeled items in the room • Author's chair • Partners/small groups • Smiling faces • Writing tool kits • Student engagement • Vocabulary list • Writing prompts • Turn and talk • Productive • Organized • Writing • Busy	• Buzz, hum, beehive • Two-inch voices • Conversation/oral language • Quiet during thinking and teaching phase • "Hum" when sharing w/ partners, triads, quads • Busy • Children making decisions • Learning is happening • Questioning	• Comfortable, natural, happy • Nonthreatening, risk taking • Purposeful • Successful • Confident • Excited • Relaxed • Proud • Comfortable sharing thoughts • "I can" attitude

Guidelines for Writer's Workshop

Standard

Understands the structure of Writer's Workshop

Materials

- *Guidelines for Writer's Workshop* (page 40; guidelineswritersws.pdf)
- Chart paper
- Markers

Mentor Texts

- *Howard B. Wigglebottom Learns to Listen* by Howard Binkow
- *No, David!* by David Shannon
- *It's Hard to Be Five* by Jamie Lee Curtis
- See *Mentor Text List* in Appendix C for other suggestions.

Procedures

Note: Repeat or reinforce this lesson until the procedure is in place. Assign partners for discussion.

Think About Writing

1. Explain to students that Writer's Workshop follows guidelines and routines in order to create a sense of order and efficiency. In Writer's Workshop, they will learn about the rigor and personal organization it takes to become a good writer.

2. Read aloud a mentor text if desired, and review the need for order and listening skills in a classroom, especially during Writer's Workshop. For example, remind students how Howard learned the importance of listening in *Howard B. Wigglebottom Learns to Listen*.

Teach

3. Tell students, "Today, we will create guidelines for Writer's Workshop." Explain that writers follow rules or guidelines during Writer's Workshop so they can make good use of their time. Tell students that since the guidelines will make them smart writers, the acronym SMART is used to help them remember the guidelines.

4. Display *Guidelines for Writer's Workshop* (page 40) or create an anchor chart with guidelines for students to follow. Adjust the guidelines as needed to fit the procedures and needs of your class. Write the guidelines on an anchor chart and post in the classroom or copy it and add to the students' writing folders.

Guidelines for Writer's Workshop (cont.)

Engage

5. Tell students they will work with partners to review the guidelines for Writer's Workshop. Explicitly model for students what they will do and say when they turn to their partners.

6. Have students *Turn and Talk* to partners about the guidelines for Writer's Workshop. Encourage students to use the anchor chart to guide their discussions. Allow two minutes for students to talk. As they talk, move from group to group and take notes on student responses.

7. Gather students back together, review the guidelines, and share your observations.

Apply

8. Remind students, "The guidelines will help us make the most of our time. The expectation for writing in this class is that the guidelines are followed so everyone in the class is able to use Writer's Workshop time well."

9. Tell students to draw a picture that shows the ideas about important writing guidelines.

Write/Conference

10. Provide students time to draw their pictures. Conferencing with students will begin once procedures are firmly in place. Help any students who need assistance get settled into the writing time. As students work, rotate around the room. Notice and compliment writing as students work. Remember to give many affirmations to your emergent authors.

Spotlight Strategy

11. Spotlight something you noticed that went well today. For example, "Jesus did something brilliant. He went to his seat and immediately started to work in his writing folder."

Share

12. Have students *Turn and Talk* to the person seated nearest them about their pictures showing the important writing guidelines. Remind students to tell why the SMART guidelines for Writer's Workshop will help them become excellent writers. Provide about two minutes for sharing.

Homework

Ask students to take a couple of minutes to think about how knowing what is expected of them will make them more disciplined (self-regulated) writers. Tell students to share their ideas with their parents.

Guidelines for Writer's Workshop

SMART Writers

Speak in two-inch voices.

Move about quietly.

Always work!

Respect others.

Tidy up.

Two-Inch Voices

Standard

Understands the structure of Writer's Workshop

Materials

- Looks Like, Sounds Like, Feels Like anchor chart (created in Managing Writer's Workshop Lesson 2, page 35)
- Marker
- Ruler

Mentor Texts

- *Howard B. Wigglebottom Learns to Listen* by Howard Binkow
- *Too Much Noise* by Ann McGovern
- See *Mentor Text List* in Appendix C for other suggestions.

Procedures

Note: Repeat or reinforce this lesson until the procedures are in place.

Think About Writing

1. Tell students that as Writer's Workshop begins moving forward, they must actively think about using a noise level that is acceptable during mini-lessons, group writing, conferring, and sharing.

2. Review a mentor text if desired, and emphasize the need for order and use of appropriate noise level in a classroom.

3. Display and review the Looks Like, Sounds Like, Feels Like anchor chart created in Managing Writer's Workshop Lesson 2 (page 35). Tell students, "Today, you will think about what Writer's Workshop time will sound like." Tell students, "When we are busy, we sometimes fail to realize that our noise level might disturb others who are writing or discussing."

Teach

4. Tell students, "Today, I will teach you about the noise level I expect you to use during our Writer's Workshop time." Explain to students that one way they can monitor their noise level is to use a two-inch voice. Show students the distance of two inches on a ruler and tell students they should speak so someone only a few inches from their mouth can hear what they are saying.

5. Model a two-inch voice that can be heard only by partners and not by others sitting close by. Turn and have a conversation with a student sitting in the group. Ask questions such as: What kind of stories do you like to write? Where do you do your best writing, home or school? What might you write about today?

Two-Inch Voices (cont.)

6. Tell students that the voice you just used was the appropriate voice level and that you will be listening for that voice level during Writer's Workshop. Revisit the anchor chart adding student insights into the *Sounds Like* section.

Engage

7. Tell students they will practice using their two-inch voices today. Give students question prompts to engage in partner conversation using two-inch voices such as, "What do we do during writing time?" "What is an interesting piece of writing you are working on?" "What did you do after school yesterday?"

8. Provide time for students to talk with their partners. Then, gather students together, and add any additional insights to the Looks Like, Sounds Like, Feels Like anchor chart.

Apply

9. Remind students that as they work today, they will use a two-inch voice as they write. This noise level will reflect respect for every writer in the room.

10. Tell students they may write or draw about the mentor text or they may use their own ideas.

Write/Conference

11. Provide time for students to write. As students write, rotate around the room making observations about student noise level. Keep notes in your Conferring Notebook. Remember to offer students many compliments about work well done.

Spotlight Strategy

12. Spotlight student work. For example, "Jenny used the exact noise level that we modeled and practiced. Did you notice the *sounds like* environment in our writing time today? That is the noise level I will be listening for during our writing time." Use this time to reinforce what Writer's Workshop will sound like and to recognize students who worked hard to practice the correct noise level today.

Share

13. Have students meet with partners for approximately two minutes and share what they worked on as writers today. As students share, observe one or two students who clearly understood the idea and have them share with the whole group.

Homework

Ask students to think about how important it is to show respect for every writer in the room by using a two-inch voice during Writer's Workshop time.

Turn and Talk

Standard

Understands the structure of Writer's Workshop

Materials

- Looks Like, Sounds Like, Feels Like anchor chart (created in Managing Writer's Workshop Lesson 2, page 35)
- Chart paper
- Markers
- *Sample Partner Conversation Chart* (page 45; partnerconversation.pdf)

Mentor Texts

- *The Worst Day of My Life Ever!* by Julia Cook
- *Personal Space Camp* by Julia Cook
- See *Mentor Text List* in Appendix C for other suggestions.

Procedures

Note: Allow students to select their own partners or assign partners based on language acquisition. The collective personality of your class should guide your decision. Repeat or reinforce this lesson until the procedure is in place.

Think About Writing

1. Explain to students that they must get routines and rituals in Writer's Workshop solid and scheduled appropriately. It is important that they talk to others about their writing. To do this, they will use a routine called *Turn and Talk*. This discussion strategy will be used throughout writing time. When students get with partners, they will talk about writing ideas and skills to become better writers.

2. Review a mentor text if desired, and emphasize the need for order and procedures in a classroom.

Teach

3. Tell students, "Today, we will practice partner conversation." Explain that when you say, "Turn and Talk," that is a signal for them to immediately turn to a person who is sitting nearby and quickly follow directions on the discussion topic.

4. Model what *Turn and Talk* should look like and sound like. Be sure to emphasize and model an appropriate two-inch voice. Then provide time for students to practice with each other.

5. Create an anchor chart with guidelines for partner conversation. Gather ideas from students about what they should do during *Turn and Talk*. Use the *Sample Partner Conversation Chart* (page 45) to guide the discussion. Be sure to explicitly talk about and list on the chart what students will do during this time.

Turn and Talk *(cont.)*

6. Tell students that when you say, "Heads-up, Stand-up, Partner-up," that is a signal that they should immediately stand up, join a partner, and make eye contact. Then, they should follow directions on the discussion topic. Model what *Heads-up, Stand-up, Partner-up* should look like and sound like. Then provide time for students to practice with each other. Praise students for their efforts.

7. Revisit the Looks Like, Sounds Like, Feels Like anchor chart, created in Managing Writer's Workshop Lesson 2 (page 35), and add student insights. Continue to add student input to this anchor chart throughout the year.

Engage

8. Tell students that now is their chance to *Turn and Talk*. Ask partners to discuss how they will be expected to conduct themselves in a *Turn and Talk*. Next, regain students' attention and have them choose new partners for a *Heads-up, Stand-up, Partner-up*. Partners should discuss what they should do during this type of partner conversation.

Apply

9. Tell students that after they write today, they will *Turn and Talk* to partners about what they have written.

Write/Conference

10. Provide time for students to write. Have students work on drafting a new piece of writing on a topic of their choice or continue with an unfinished piece from their folder. As students write, rotate around the room making observations about student noise level. Keep notes in your Conferring Notebook. Remember to offer students many compliments about work well done.

Spotlight Strategy

11. There is no specific spotlighting strategy today. Celebrating is done through the actual *Turn and Talk* and *Heads-up, Stand-up, Partner-up*.

Share

12. Gather students together to share their work. Have students *Turn and Talk* to partners for two minutes to share their writing. Then, call a *Heads-up, Stand-up, Partner-up* and have students choose a new partner with whom to share their writing.

Homework

Ask students to think about how *Turn and Talk* and *Heads-up, Stand-up, Partner-up* conversations energize writing ideas. Also, ask them to think about how important it is to show respect for every writer in the room by using a two-inch voice.

Sample Partner Conversation Chart

- Find your partner quickly.

- Use a soft, two-inch voice.

- Make eye contact with your partner.

- Stick to the writing topic.

- Ask questions to clarify thinking.

- Make sure each partner has a turn to talk.

- Give a compliment when needed.

- Only "put-ups"—NO "put-downs."

Posture and Pencil Grip

Procedures

Note: Repeat or reinforce this lesson until the procedure is in place. This lesson will begin with a group meeting. Students will then move to their seats for practice with pencil grip and posture.

Think About Writing

1. Remind students about the classroom expectations for Writer's Workshop by reviewing the anchor charts they helped create. Tell students they will continue to practice following Writer's Workshop guidelines and begin learning about how authors write.

2. Review the mentor text if desired, and emphasize the need for students to listen in a classroom.

Teach

3. Tell students, "Today, I will share two important ideas you must understand to be successful writers: pencil grip and posture." Tell students that writers sit with good posture in an upright position so that oxygen can flow to the brain. Model how to sit up tall with the chair pushed in and both feet on the floor.

4. Explain that writers also hold the pencil correctly. One way to pick up the pencil so it is held correctly is to *Pinch and Roll* the pencil. Model the following steps several times for students.

   - Begin with the pencil on the desk so the lead is pointing toward you.
   - Pinch the pencil with your thumb and pointer finger.
   - Flip the pencil backwards so it is cupped softly between the curve of the thumb and the pointer finger. The pencil should rest gently on the middle finger. When placed correctly, the pencil will be placed with the thumb on one side of the pencil, pointer on top of the pencil, and the middle finger gently supporting the pencil.

Posture and Pencil Grip *(cont.)*

5. Have students pretend to be at their desks and use an imaginary pencil to practice *Pinch and Roll* to get their pencils in the correct position. Repeat several times as needed.

Engage

6. Have students move to their desks to practice pencil grip and posture with their partners. Encourage students to provide support to their partners as they get the feel of proper posture and pencil grip.

Apply

7. Ask students to practice the proper posture and pencil grip as they write. Tell them this will help as they practice letter formation and begin writing letters, words, sentences, and stories.

Write/Conference

8. Provide time for students to draw, sketch, or write about a topic of their choice for three to five minutes. As they work, rotate among students and make observations about posture and pencil grip. Keep notes in your Conferring Notebook and offer lots of praise.

Spotlight Strategy

9. Spotlight student work. For example, "What brilliant writers you are. You have already taken ownership of this important writing time. Notice how Kim sits with the correct posture." Choose several students to model correct posture and pencil grip. Remember to use this time to celebrate successes.

Share

10. Have students meet with partners to share what they wrote today. Provide approximately two minutes for partners to talk. From teacher observations, choose one or two students who clearly understood the idea and have them share with the whole group.

Homework

Ask students to think about how important it is to use correct posture and pencil grip. Have them tell their parents about this important learning. Tell them to be ready to practice posture and pencil grip tomorrow when they return to workshop time.

Sharing

Standard

Understands the structure of Writer's Workshop

Materials

- Looks Like, Sounds Like, Feels Like anchor chart (created in Managing Writer's Workshop Lesson 2, page 35)
- *I Like/I Wonder Cards* (page 50; likewondercards.pdf)

Mentor Texts

- *Me First* by Helen Lester
- *We Share Everything* by Robert Munsch
- See *Mentor Text List* in Appendix C for other suggestions.

Procedures

Note: Repeat or reinforce this lesson until the procedure is in place, consistent, and automatic. Sharing may take place in the meeting area or at student desks. The *I Like/ I Wonder Cards* (page 50) can be distributed later in the year if desired.

Think About Writing

1. Remind students about the classroom expectations for Writer's Workshop by reviewing the Looks Like, Sounds Like, Feels Like anchor chart created in Managing Writer's Workshop Lesson 2 (page 35). Tell students that today, they will learn about an important step of Writer's Workshop—sharing. Explain that sharing their writing gives them a chance to hear what others are writing and to share their own writing.

2. Review a mentor text if desired, and emphasize the need to be respectful to others and share.

Teach

3. Tell students, "Today, I will show you how to meet with classmates to share your writing." Explain that share time will be at the end of Writer's Workshop. Tell students that they will have three to five minutes to share their writing. Sometimes sharing will take place with a large group and sometimes in smaller groups.

4. Tell students that when they talk with others, it is important that everyone works together. One person will share what he or she has written. The other person(s) must be a good listener(s) and respond to the writing.

5. Explain that responding to writing is an important job and must be done with care. Display the *I Like/I Wonder Cards.* Tell students that the words *I like* will remind them to give a compliment about the person's writing. Model making several compliments. Then, tell students that the words *I wonder* will remind them to ask a question about the person's writing. Model asking several questions.

Sharing (cont.)

6. Tell students they will practice forming smaller groups to share. Explain to students that when you tell them to meet with partners, they should move quickly to find a partner and begin sharing. Show students how you will raise one finger at a time to count to five. Explain that you expect students to be with a partner by the time you get to five.

7. Model finding a partner for students. Then, have them practice several times until the routine is firmly in place.

8. Explain to students there will be times you want them to share in triads (3) or quads (4). Model forming triads and quads and then have students practice forming these groups as well. You may wish to practice forming triads and quads on other days.

9. Revisit the Looks Like, Sounds Like, Feels Like anchor chart, adding student insights from Writer's Workshop.

Engage

10. Tell students to *Heads-up, Stand-up, Partner- up*. Tell them to talk with their partner about what they will do when they share their writing at the end of Writer's Workshop. Praise students for forming groups quickly and sharing their ideas.

Apply

11. Tell students that meeting with a partner, triad, or quad at the end of writing time allows them to have an audience for all their hard writing work. Remind them that they will give compliments and ask questions about other students' writing.

Write/Conference

12. Provide time for students to write. Have students continue to work from their folders. All students should write every day, even when mini-lessons focus on management.

Spotlight Strategy

13. Spotlight strategies will take place during the sharing component of the lesson.

Share

14. Tell students they will practice the important procedures for share time. Provide students with *I Like/I Wonder Cards* to use while they meet with partners and to keep in their writing folders. Tell students to take their writing and meet with a partner. Use your fingers to count to five. Allow for one minute of share time. Remind students to give compliments and ask questions about their partners' writing. Then have students meet with a quad. Finally, have students meet with a triad. Provide compliments and praise for sharing that is well done.

Homework

Ask students to think about how they met in partners, triads, and quads. Tell students to share with their parents how they will share their writing with classmates and the kind of compliment they might give and receive. Remind them to practice the language of compliments.

I Like/I Wonder Cards

Teacher Directions: Create copies of this sheet. Cut out the cards and distribute them to students according to the directions in the lesson.

Print Concepts
Connecting Writing to Reading

Students begin first grade with a wide range of understanding of print concepts. Although most should have a good understanding of print concepts, depending on their kindergarten writing experiences, there may be some gaps in their knowledge. Early exposure to print concepts in writing assists students in making the connections needed to develop early literacy skills. Print concept lessons should be taught early in the year. Once the initial lessons have been taught, work with small groups of students who are still having difficulty with particular concepts. Check in with those students during Writing/Conferencing time to assist them as they write. Lessons on print concepts include:

- Lesson 1: Connecting Sounds to Names (page 53)
- Lesson 2: Where to Start! Left to Right and Return Sweep (page 55)
- Lesson 3: Directionality and Lowercase Letters (page 57)
- Lesson 4: Spacing (page 61)

Connecting Sounds to Names

Standard

Uses conventions of print in writing

Materials

- Chart paper
- Marker
- *Classroom Names* (page 34; classroomnames.pdf)
- *My Hand Plan* (page 141; myhandplan.pdf)

Mentor Texts

- *A, My Name Is Alice* by Jane E. Bayer
- Any alphabet book
- See *Mentor Text List* in Appendix C for other suggestions.

Procedures

Note: Pay close attention to students who need additional practice in using writing tools in a small group or individually. Helping these students to use these tools effectively will help them be more independent during Writer's Workshop.

Think About Writing

1. Explain to students that they will build writing stamina, or "muscle," and learn to sustain writing for longer periods of time during Writer's Workshop.

2. Review a mentor text if desired, and emphasize how each letter of the alphabet relates to the item(s) on the pages.

Teach

3. Tell students, "Today, I will show you how to listen to the names of our classmates and use the letters in their names to write words. If you want to write a word but you are not sure what letters to use, *Classroom Names* (page 34) is a tool that can help you."

4. Display *Classroom Names* and model how to use it to find initial sound spellings. Say a simple phrase or sentence, such as, "The dog jumps." Model how to use *Classroom Names* to identify the first letter of each word: "Dog—that starts with *d* like Deena." Find *Deena* on the name chart and point out the letter *D*. Then, "Jumps starts like Jamal." Find *Jamal* on the name chart and point out the letter *J*. Write *The dog jumps* on chart paper and point out the initial letters.

Connecting Sounds to Names (cont.)

Engage

5. Have students think of something they would like to write about. Encourage them to think of words that begin like the names of students in the classroom. Tell students to *Heads-up, Stand-up, Partner-up*. Have them share what they will write about with their partner. Provide approximately three minutes for students to share. As students share, move around, listen, and find something to praise.

Apply

6. Allow time for students to plan what they will write. If you have taught them how to rehearse their stories using their fingers *My Hand Plan* (page 141), encourage them to use that strategy. Remind students to refer back to the name chart for beginning sound help while writing.

Write/Conference

7. Provide time for students to write. As students write, rotate around the room talking with students about their writing. Keep notes in your Conferring Notebook. Remember to offer students many compliments about work well done.

Spotlight Strategy

8. Spotlight student work. Make a point to spotlight students when you see them using the name chart. For example, "Chloe is using the classroom name chart to support her writing efforts. Smart writing work! Good writers use all the tools around them to help them write their important words."

Share

9. Have students meet with partners and share what they wrote today. Remind students they may give a compliment or ask a question to their partners.

Homework

Ask students to make a list of five words that begin with the same letter as their names. Tell them to be ready to share their lists in Writer's Workshop.

Where to Start! Left to Right and Return Sweep

Standard

Uses conventions of print in writing

Materials

- Chart paper
- Markers
- Mini stickers
- *My Hand Plan* (page 141; myhandplan.pdf)

Mentor Texts

- *ABC I Like Me!* by Nancy Carlson
- Any early level reading book with the print beginning at the top of the page and at least two lines of print on each page.
- See *Mentor Text List* in Appendix C for other suggestions.

Procedures

Note: You may wish to teach return sweep as a separate mini-lesson based on the developmental needs of your students.

Thinking About Writing

1. Tell students that the class is a community of writers where all ideas are valued. Remind students that they are all authors, just like authors who write books for them to read.

2. Review a mentor text if desired, and emphasize the direction you are reading.

Teach

3. Tell students, "Today I will show you where to begin writing, which way to move across the page, and how to return to the next line of print." Explain to students that authors always begin their stories on the left side of the page and write across the page to the right. Place a sticker on the left side of a sheet of chart paper to show where to begin writing. Draw an arrow towards the right so students know which direction they should move when writing. This is also a time to reteach left and right hands.

4. Tell students if they get to the end of the line and have more to write, they should return to the beginning of the next line. Continue the arrow you drew in step three to the end of the line and return it to the beginning of the next line.

5. Tell students that sometimes it is easier to write a story after drawing a picture. Draw a simple picture to write about.

Where to Start! Left to Right and Return Sweep *(cont.)*

6. Place another sticker on a new line on the left side of the sheet of chart paper, just below your picture. Write a sentence about the picture. Make the sentence long enough that you can show the return sweep to the next line.

Engage

7. Ask students to think about something they will write about today. Have students *Turn and Talk* to partners and share their ideas. Encourage students to rehearse what they will write over their fingers if you have taught that mini-lesson (*My Hand Plan*, page 141). Allow two minutes of oral rehearsal/talk time. Gather students together on the carpet.

Apply

8. Have students use their fingers to show the direction they will write as they move across the page. Remind students that if they need more space to write, they can return to the beginning of the next line.

9. Provide students with mini stickers. Tell them when they begin writing today, they will place their mini stickers on the left side of the page where they will begin writing.

Write/Conference

10. Provide time for students to write. You may want to keep a small group of students who need to practice writing left to right and return sweep for additional time with this mini lesson. Then, once all students are working, rotate around the room, talking with students about their writing. Keep notes in your Conferring Notebook. Remember to offer students many compliments about work well done.

Spotlight Strategy

11. Spotlight student's use of left to right and return sweep. For example, "Gabriel began writing his story in the correct spot and is writing across the page, just like an author. When he got to the end of the line, he moved down to a new line of print. Smart writing work!"

Share

12. Have two or three students share their writing. Select students who began their writing at the sticker, moved across the page from left to right, and moved to a new line of print.

Homework
Ask students to make a list of five ideas they can use for writing topics.

Directionality and Lowercase Letters

Standard

Uses conventions of print in writing

Materials

- Chart paper
- Marker
- *Making Letters* (pages 59–60; makingletters.pdf)
- *Classroom Names* (page 34; classroomnames.pdf)

Mentor Texts

- *Alphabet Adventure* by Audrey and Bruce Wood
- *Alphabet City* by Stephen Johnson
- See *Mentor Text List* in Appendix C for other suggestions.

Procedures

Note: Repeat this lesson over several days until students are forming letters correctly, moving top to bottom and left to right. Consider spending at least one day on stick letters, one day on circle letters, and one day on special letters. Also, as you model writing, review correct posture and pencil grip.

Think About Writing

1. Explain to students that writers learn to form letters correctly so they can focus on writing rather than how to form the letters. Writers who move their hands in an awkward position sometimes develop print confusions about how writing works.

2. Review a mentor text if desired, and emphasize the direction you are reading as well as lowercase letters in the book.

Teach

3. Tell students, "Today, I will show you how to form your letters correctly." Use letter chants from *Making Letters* (pages 59–60). Use the following steps for each letter you practice:

   - Model writing a letter on a sheet of chart paper as you say the chant. Students echo the chant.
   - Have students move their whole hands in the air to practice the proper stroke for the letter.
   - Have students use their index fingers to write the letter in the air or on the carpet or desk.

4. Repeat the steps to practice each of the letters you have designated for today's lesson. Consider using *Classroom Names* (page 34) to allow students more practice writing letters.

Directionality and Lowercase Letters (cont.)

Engage

5. Tell students to *Turn and Talk* and use their fingers to demonstrate letter movement to their partner. Students should sit facing in the same direction, not facing each other. Encourage partners to watch directionality and check for accuracy.

Apply

6. Remind students as they write to start on the left side of their papers and to use the correct letter formation. Tell students they may write about their parents, friends, toys, or one of their own ideas.

Write/Conference

7. Provide time for students to write. As students work, rotate around the room having conversations with students about their writing. Keep notes in your Conferring Notebook. Remember to offer students many compliments about work well done.

Spotlight Strategy

8. Spotlight good writing. For example, "Smart writing work today. You must be very proud of the direction you are moving to form letters correctly. Connor is practicing and saying the letter movement. Brilliant work!"

Share

9. Have students meet with partners to share the writing they did today. Remind students to compliment their partners on their writing.

Homework

Tell students their hands go with them wherever they go. Ask students to practice letter formation of the letters in their names using the palms of their hands and fingers. Have students tell their parents about their important writing work.

Making Letters

Stick Family

l "tall stick down"

t "tall stick down and then across"

f "hook stick down and then across"

b "tall stick down, back up and around"

h "tall stick down and then a hump"

m "short stick down, then two humps"

n "short stick down, then one hump"

r "short stick down, then half a hump"

p "long stick down, back up and around"

i "short stick down, and then a dot"

j "curly stick down, and then a dot"

k "tall stick down, then in and out"

Making Letters (cont.)

Circle Family

c   "up and around"

o   "up and all the way around"

a   "up and all the way around, then a straight stick down"

d   "up and all the way around, then a tall stick down"

g   "up, around, then a curly stick down"

q   "up, around, then a curly stick out"

s   "up, around, then curl back around"

e   "straight stick across, then up, and around"

Special Family

u   "down, around, up and short stick down"

v   "down, up"

w   "down, up, down up"

x   "criss-cross"

y   "short stick down, then long stick down"

z   "straight across, down, across"

Spacing

Standard
Uses conventions of print in writing

Materials
- Chart paper
- Markers
- Word spacers

Mentor Texts
- Any level B or C book with clear word boundaries
- See *Mentor Text List* in Appendix C for other suggestions.

Procedures

Note: Students will need word spacers for the lesson. Students can use erasers, clothes pins, or scrap strips of paper with stickers on the end. Also, commercial word spacers are available for purchase.

Think About Writing

1. Remind students that they have been learning about how Writer's Workshop works and practicing thinking like an author. Explain that young writers have to learn how each word needs empty space around it so that writing is not jumbled together. Sometimes we write for ourselves and sometimes we write information for others to read. When we write for others, spacing helps the reader understand our words.

2. Review a mentor text if desired, and emphasize the spacing between words.

Teach

3. Tell students, "Today, I will show you how I use a spacer to build empty space around each word so my reader will understand my message." Write a sentence on chart paper. Read the sentence to students several times. Hold the word spacer between each word as you read the sentence to show students the space created between words. Tell students this space separates the words to make it easier to read.

4. Model creating a sentence using the word spacer. Write the sentence *I love to read books* on chart paper. Write according to your student audience (sound out and phonetically spell words as necessary). Emphasize the spaces between the words by using the word spacer.

5. Create emphasis by rereading your sentence several times and showing the spacing.

Spacing *(cont.)*

Engage

6. Tell students to *Heads-up, Stand-up, Partner-up* and talk about what they will write today. You may want to talk with an exaggerated space after each word as you give the directions in order to emphasize word boundaries. Provide approximately two minutes for partners to talk.

Apply

7. Provide students with space holders. Remind students to leave some empty space around each word as they write.

Write/Conference

8. Provide time for students to write. As students write, determine if any students need additional support or reteaching on the concept of spacing. Keep those students for an additional mini-lesson on spacing between words. Then, once all students are working, rotate around the room having conversations with students about their writing. Keep notes in your Conferring Notebook. Remember to offer students many compliments about work well done.

Spotlight Strategy

9. Spotlight good spacing. For example, "Camila is saying each word slowly, and using a spacer to show she is ready to move to the next word. What marvelous writers! You are using important writing rules as you all write."

Share

10. Select several students who used correct spacing in their writing to showcase. For example, "I want you each to see how Mark, Tracy, and Brandon used a spacer to show empty space around each word. Turn and look at today's spotlighted authors."

Homework

Ask students to look for evidence of spacing in print around their houses. Have them bring a book to school to share with their partners. Tell them to be ready to show the spacing between words in the book with partners tomorrow during Writer's Workshop.

Ideas

Thinking, Thinking, Thinking!

Ideas are the heart of writing. The purpose of this section is to help students generate ideas for writing. The lessons assist students to explore the ideas of authors using mentor texts, and to discover unique writing ideas in their own lives. Through class-created anchor charts and individually-created lists, students will collect plenty of ideas, so that when they begin to write, they are not at a loss for topics. Students are encouraged to keep their ideas in their writing folders so the ideas are readily at hand. Lessons in this section include the following:

- Lesson 1: Ideas Thinking Chart (page 65)
- Lesson 2: My Idea Bank (page 67)
- Lesson 3: Getting Ideas from Literature (page 70)
- Lesson 4: Kings and Queens of Writing (page 72)
- Lesson 5: My Expert List (page 74)
- Lesson 6: Places I Love (page 77)
- Lesson 7: People I Love (page 80)

The *Ida, Idea Creator* poster (page 64) can be displayed in the room to provide a visual reminder for students that creating Ideas is one of the traits of writing. You may wish to introduce this poster during the first lesson on ideas. Then, refer to the poster when teaching other lessons on ideas to refresh students' memories and provide them with questions to help hone their writing topics.

Ida
Idea Creator

What is my writing about?

✔ Did I choose an interesting topic?

✔ Did I focus on my idea?

✔ Did I include supporting details?

✔ Did I stick to my topic?

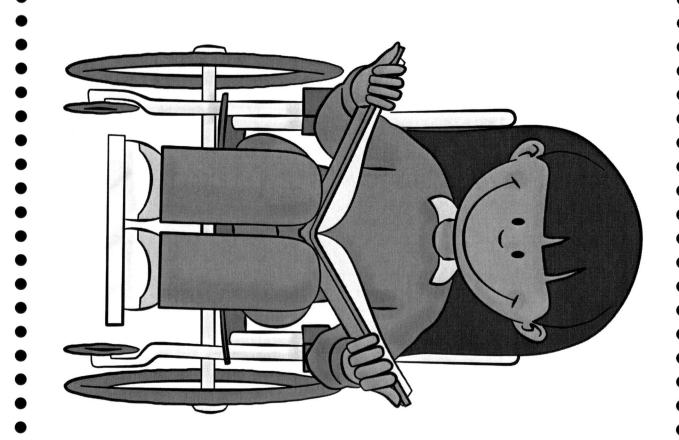

Ideas Thinking Chart

Standard

Uses prewriting strategies to plan written work

Materials

- Chart paper
- Markers

Mentor Texts

- *Chrysanthemum* by Kevin Henkes
- See *Mentor Text List* in Appendix C for other suggestions.

Procedures

Note: This mini-lesson may be repeated monthly to support students with ideas and words for writing. The possibilities are endless and may include: school words, people we love, words for fall. The ideas on the chart also serve as a word bank.

Think About Writing

1. Tell students that we need to develop and keep lists of important ideas that can be used to write stories. Writers should continue to add to their list so they always have topics to explore in their writing.

2. Review a mentor text, and emphasize that authors have many different ideas that they can choose from when they write.

Teach

3. Tell students, "Today, I will show you how to make a list of ideas you can use when writing." Explain that they will help create a class list of ideas to write about, but they can also keep their own idea list in their writing folders. Write the title *Writing Ideas* at the top of a sheet of chart paper.

4. Remind students that they have been reading books about our first days in school and talking about the things we do at school. Add the word *school* to the chart. Draw a simple picture next to the word to support word meaning.

5. Tell students that you know they have lots of friends at school. Add the word *friend* to the chart along with a picture to support understanding. Model other words if needed before proceeding to the next step.

Ideas Thinking Chart (cont.)

Engage

6. Tell students to *Heads-up, Stand-up, Partner-up* and share something they like to do at school. Provide time for students to share with each other. Then, have them share their ideas out loud as you add the ideas to the chart.

Apply

7. Tell students that you heard wonderful ideas that they can use in stories. Share a few responses and give affirmations. Remind students new ideas can be added to the chart.

Write/Conference

8. Provide time for students to write. As students work, rotate around the room having conversations with students about their writing. Keep notes in your Conferring Notebook. Remember to offer students many compliments about work well done.

Spotlight Strategy

9. Spotlight a student who has turned a creative idea into a story. For example, "Excellent work ethic. Maria went to work writing a brilliant story. Amazing writing work today. You are to be commended."

Share

10. Choose three students to come share their writing in the Author's Chair. Provide affirmation for the work they share.

Homework

Ask students to think about all the ideas the class listed on the *Writing Ideas* chart. Ask them to make a list of three ideas from the class chart and three personal ideas they would like to use as writing topics.

My Idea Bank

Standard
Uses prewriting strategies to plan written work

Materials
- Magazines and newspapers
- A picture from home
- *Idea Bank Cards* (page 69; ideabankcards.pdf)
- Sheet protectors
- Coins and piggy bank

Mentor Texts
- *Wallace's Lists* by Barbara Bottner
- See *Mentor Text List* in Appendix C for other suggestions.

Procedures
Note: Photocopy the *Idea Bank Cards* (page 69) and cut into fourths. Place the *Idea Bank Cards* in a place in the classroom where students can access them as needed.

Think About Writing
1. Tell students that each time authors write, they start with an idea. Ideas are like coins. Each one we add increases the amount in our bank. Demonstrate dropping coins into a piggy bank. We drop the coins into our bank and save them until we need something special. In the same way, good writers gather ideas and save them for their special stories.

2. Review a mentor text with students, and emphasize that authors have many ideas that they can choose from when they write.

Teach
3. Remind students that they helped create a class idea chart. Tell students, "Today, I will show you how to create a collection of ideas you are interested in using in your writing." Tell students this will be their *Idea Bank*—a place where they can save ideas they may want to use for writing.

4. Explain that one way they can save their ideas is to draw a picture. Model how to draw a picture on an *Idea Bank Card*. Remember to label the picture. Place the *Idea Bank Card* in a sheet protector and put it in a writing folder.

My Idea Bank (cont.)

5. Explain that their *Idea Bank* can come in other forms, too. They can collect pictures from a magazine or newspaper that might be an interesting idea for writing. Show students a photograph or picture you have cut out from a magazine. Share a personal experience related to the picture. For example, "Saturday, I happened to glance out the window and a gorgeous rainbow stretched from my Granny's house across the highway to my daughter's house. I rushed outside and took a picture. I will put that picture in my *Idea Bank*." Place the photograph in the sheet protector.

Engage

6. Have students *Turn and Talk* with partners about something they might want to take a picture of to build their *Idea Banks*. Set a timer and monitor students for focused discussions. (You might want to keep a digital camera in the classroom to build a class *Idea Bank*.)

Apply

7. Remind students that when we need to buy something, we get money from our bank. In the same way, when we need an idea for writing, we can get it from our *Idea Bank*. Tell students that the need for ideas is ongoing and they should always be on the lookout for ideas to add to their *Idea Banks*.

Write/Conference

8. Tell students they will use their writing time to think of ideas to add to their *Idea Bank*. Make magazines or newspapers and *Idea Bank Cards* available to students as they gather ideas. Provide students with sheet protectors to save their writing ideas.

9. Rotate around the room conferring with students as they record their ideas. Possible conferring questions to ask incude: "What are ideas that you want to place in your *Idea Bank*? How will this help you become proficient at developing ideas?"

Spotlight Strategy

10. Point out examples of students who quickly moved into their activity and knew exactly how to find/make ideas to drop into their bank.

Share

11. Have students meet with partners and share other ways or places they can collect ideas for their Idea Banks.

Homework

Ask students to bring five photographs, magazine ideas, or newspaper clippings that they want to place in their *Idea Banks*. Have them share their ideas with their parents.

Idea Bank Cards

Teacher Directions: Create copies of this sheet. Cut out the cards and distribute them to students according to the directions in the lesson.

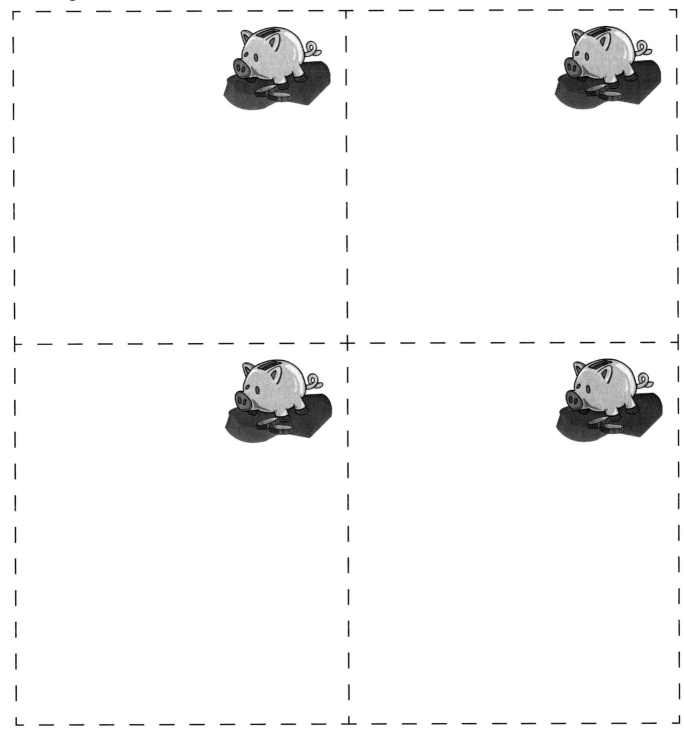

Getting Ideas from Literature

Standard

Uses prewriting strategies to plan written work

Materials

- Chart paper
- Markers
- *Ideas from Literature* (Appendix D, page 271)

Mentor Texts

- *Knuffle Bunny* by Mo Willems
- See *Mentor Text List* in Appendix C for other suggestions.

Procedures

Note: This mini-lesson uses *Knuffle Bunny* for specific examples; however, the idea behind the lesson can be used with numerous texts by connecting the topic or writing craft used by the author. See *Ideas from Literature* list in Appendix D (page 271) for additional book titles and suggested connections. Students enjoy writing like the author. Provide multiple opportunuties with rich literature.

Think About Writing

1. Tell students that authors often get ideas for writing their own stories by reading literature. We can learn about how to get ideas by looking at what book authors write about. For example, in the book *Knuffle Bunny*, Mo Willems shows how the things we do in our daily lives, like running simple errands or doing the laundry, can become a story. Mr. Willems also uses illustrations to show how we might create stories from our daily routine. In this book, notice the title, the picture of the child, and the bunny. They will play a significant role in this story.

Teach

2. Tell students, "Today, I will show you how to explore literature to create ideas for your own stories." Tell students, "I read a book in which a girl went to the laundromat with her father. I think I will write about going shopping at the store with my mom." Quickly draw a picture of a car and shopping cart on a sheet of chart paper.

3. Expand the idea of going to a store into a longer story and write it on chart paper. For example, "Mom loved to shop. She rode in a little electric cart. I had to push the basket." Tell students that when you write stories on paper, you can share the idea with others and keep the memories alive forever.

Getting Ideas from Literature (cont.)

4. Tell students you will reread the story to make certain that the writing looks right, sounds right, and makes sense according to your thinking.

Engage

5. Ask students to think of a simple chore they do with their families. Have them *Turn and Talk* to partners and expand that one idea. Have students plan what they will write by rehearsing their stories using their fingers as done previously. Provide approximately three minutes of talking time.

Apply

6. Remind students how important it is to understand that writing is all around us and used in our lives every day. It is more important than watching TV or playing video games. Writing helps us to store our memories so that we can pull them out years from now, recover the important things that have happened in our lives, and hold them close to us. Our memories can be funny or sad, but they still are our memories. Tell students that as they write, they are saving their memories.

Write/Conference

7. Provide time for students to write. As students work, have conversations with students about their writing. Support their efforts in expanding ideas into longer stories. Ask questions, such as " What are you working on as a writer?" "How is your writing going today?" Keep notes in your Conferring Notebook. Remember to offer students compliments about their work.

Spotlight Strategy

8. Spotlight a student who has used an idea from literature to create a story. For example, "Sophia has taken an idea from an author and turned it into her own story."

Share

9. Have students meet with a new writing partner and share ideas that they learned from Mo Willems or the author you used as an example in the mini-lesson. Think of all the wonderful ideas you can gather from literature. Provide approximately two minutes for students to share. Remind students to always read and listen with writing in mind.

Homework

Ask students to look around their houses for different ways people write. Tell them to make a list of five ways people use writing in their houses. Ask students to be prepared to share their lists in Writer's Workshop tomorrow.

Kings and Queens of Writing

Standard

Uses prewriting strategies to plan written work

Materials

- Chart paper
- Marker
- 8.5" × 11" paper

Mentor Texts

- *I Like Myself!* By Karen Beaumont
- *A, My Name is Alice* by Jane E. Bayer
- *ABC I Like Me!* by Nancy Carlson
- See *Mentor Text List* in Appendix C for other suggestions.

Procedures

Note: You may wish to have students draw their prewriting, especially early in the school year. Allowing students to draw allows them to get their ideas on paper without the anxiety of having to write. Once the ideas are drawn on paper, students can focus on the task of writing.

Think About Writing

1. Remind students that they have all been working together and becoming a successful community of writers. Tell them they know how to generate ideas, are learning how to spell words correctly, and can write great sentences. Explain that authors write many of their stories about the people, places, and things that are special in their lives.

2. Tell students they will become kings and queens of writing ideas. Review a mentor text, and emphasize the book's focus on the individual. For example, in *I Like Myself!*, the author strongly states that no matter how she feels on the inside or looks on the outside, she is satisfied because "She is ME!"

Teach

3. Tell students, "Today I will show you how to use what is special about you to get ideas for writing." Tell students that in their kingdoms, they reside as a king or queen. Ask the kings and queens about some of their favorite or special things. For example: "Do you have special pets? What do you like to eat? What is your favorite color? Who are the special people in your life?" Continue providing other suggestions as they relate to your specific group of students.

4. Demonstrate how to fold a sheet of 8.5" × 11" paper in half so it is 8.5" × 5.5". Hold the paper so it opens like a book. Tell students that today, you are the Queen (or King) of Writing Ideas. Make a quick sketch of yourself wearing a crown on the front of a folded paper.

Kings and Queens of Writing (cont.)

5. Open up the paper. Inside, create a web map. Write your name in the center of the paper and draw a circle around it. Around the outside of the circle, write other words that tell about you. Draw circles around those words and connect them back to the circle with your name in the center of the paper. Remind students that all the ideas on the page should be about themselves.

6. Tell students they will practice being kings and queens of writing.

Engage

7. Tell students to *Heads-up, Stand-up, Partner-up* and share their ideas about their "kingdoms" (lives). Encourage students to share at least five ideas. Have them use their five fingers as a reminder about how many things they have shared. Model how to share their ideas. Tell students, "As you share, expand on each idea with a little more information. After you share each idea, hold up one finger. When you have all five fingers of one hand up, it is your partner's turn." Provide approximately three minutes for students to share.

Apply

8. Remind students they have stories to share about the special people, places, and things in their lives. Encourage students to create an interesting collection of king's and queen's information as they work today.

Write/Conference

9. Provide students with blank paper to create their webs. Keep yourself free to roam, praise, comment, and observe as students write. If problems arise, see those students immediately so they are not wasting important time. Make notes of observations in your Conferring Notebook.

Spotlight Strategy

10. Spotlight a student who created a great web. For example, "Alicia created a great kingdom web about herself. Amazing effort!"

Share

11. Have students share the ideas they wrote about their kingdoms. Ask students to take this opportunity to look closely at their writing and share their ideas with a writing friend.

Homework

Ask students to share their king or queen ideas at home. Then, have them make a list of five ideas to add to their king or queen of the kingdom papers tomorrow.

My Expert List

Standard
Uses prewriting strategies to plan written work

Materials
- Chart paper
- Markers
- *My Expert List* (page 76; myexpertlist.pdf)

Mentor Texts
- *Wallace's Lists* by Barbara Bottner
- *I Can Write!* by Theo LeSieg
- See *Mentor Text List* in Appendix C for other suggestions.

Procedures

Note: Post *My Expert List* (page 76) that you create in this lesson so that students can view it and add their own ideas about expertise. Use ideas from any author and include ideas for "how to do something." For example, how to make sandwiches, feed pets, etc. Repeat this lesson periodically.

Think About Writing

1. Tell students that one way writers get ideas is from experiences in their lives.

2. Review a mentor text if desired, and emphasize the lists in the book. For example, in *Wallace's List*, Wallace makes lists of: *Things To Do, Accidents that Happened to Me, Places with Funny Names*, and *Things I Hate.* Tell students that lists about our lives can become the sparks that ignite our writing. Every writer needs a place to gather ideas that inspire.

Teach

3. Tell students, "Today, I will show you how to create an expert list so that you always have an idea that you can weave into a story." Explain that you know there are things the students are very good at doing. Tell students that those ideas can be placed on an expert list. Ideas from this list can be turned into stories.

4. Create a class expert list. Write the title *My Expert List* at the top of a sheet of chart paper. Then write the sentence starter, "We can write about…" Write several examples of things you are good at doing (e.g., riding a bike, making a cake, etc.). Allow students to chime in with ideas of things to add to the list.

Engage

5. Have students *Turn and Talk* with partners about things they can write on their expert list of ideas. Allow approximately two minutes for partners to talk with each other.

My Expert List (cont.)

Apply

6. Tell students that they will begin creating their expert lists today. Explain that it is important to continually update their lists and add new important experiences so that their lists of writing ideas are endless.

Write/Conference

7. Distribute *My Expert List* to students. Have them write for 5–10 minutes. As students work, rotate around the room having conversations with students about their lists. Ask questions such as: How will creating this expert list help you with your writing? Keep notes in your Conferring Notebook. Remember to offer students many compliments about work well done.

Spotlight Strategy

8. Spotlight a student with an interesting expert list. For example, "Writers, excellent expert lists! You are amazing writers! Mason has already added several ideas to his growing list."

Share

9. Have students meet with writing partners to share at least three items from their lists. Remind students to compliment and ask questions about their partner's lists.

Homework

Provide students with an extra copy of *My Expert List*. Ask students to take the list home and write at least three ideas that can be added to their writing folder's expert list.

Name: _____ Date: _____

My Expert List

Directions: Make a list of the things you know that you can write about.

I can write about...

☐ _____

☐ _____

☐ _____

☐ _____

☐ _____

☐ _____

☐ _____

☐ _____

☐ _____

☐ _____

#50915—Core of Writing—Level 1   © Shell Education

Places I Love

Procedures

Note: This lesson may be split into two days. On day one, develop a whole-class anchor chart and have students develop individual charts. Then on day two, have students develop ideas about one special place. Have students store their ideas in the green dot side of their writing folders.

Think About Writing

1. Tell students it is important to accumulate lots of ideas so that the time they spend in Writer's Workshop will be wisely spent writing about their own experiences. We all have memories and images stored away in our heads and hearts about special places that bring our own personal connection to that place.

2. Review a mentor text if desired, and emphasize ways to gather ideas for writing. For example, each page in Patricia MacLachlan's *All the Places to Love* carries us on a journey to a special place.

Teach

3. Tell students, "Today I will show you how to get inspiration for writing from the places you have visited." Begin an anchor chart by writing the title *Places I Love* at the top of a sheet of chart paper. Tell students special places can be simple, such as, a tree limb, a special hiding place under the stairs, a swing in a grove of trees. Record several examples of places that are special to you. Encourage students to add ideas to the class list. Tell students this list of special places can provide ideas they can use in stories that they write.

4. Model how to choose one idea from the *Places I Love* (page 79) list and make a new list by thinking of at least three details about the place.

Standard

Uses prewriting strategies to plan written work

Materials

- Chart paper
- Markers
- *Places I Love* (page 79; placesilove.pdf)

Mentor Texts

- *All the Places to Love* by Patricia MacLachlan
- See *Mentor Text List* in Appendix C for other suggestions.

Places I Love (cont.)

Engage

5. Have students *Turn and Talk* with partners and talk about places they know and may want to use in their writing.

Apply

6. Tell students that they will begin creating their own *Places I Love* list today. Explain that it is important to constantly update their lists and add new important places so that their lists of writing ideas are endless.

Write/Conference

7. Distribute *Places I Love* (page 79) to students. Have them write for 5–10 minutes. As students work, rotate around the room having conversations with students about their lists. Keep notes in your Conferring Notebook so that you will know whether to revisit this lesson or move ahead. Remember to offer students many compliments about work well done.

Spotlight Strategy

8. Spotlight a student who listed interesting places. For example, "You must be so proud of your excellent places." And, "Sanjay quickly sketched an important place and is ready to make a story about that very special place. Superb thinking today!" Spotlight one or two students.

Share

9. Have students meet in triads to share what they accomplished in writing today. Remind students to pay a compliment or ask a question of each person who shares ideas.

Homework

Ask students to think of places that excite or motivate them and make them want to tell someone. Have students make a list of three places they would like to write about. Tell them to be ready to share their ideas tomorrow.

Name: _____ Date: _____

Places I Love

Directions: Make a list of the places that you love.

☐ _____

☐ _____

☐ _____

☐ _____

☐ _____

☐ _____

☐ _____

☐ _____

☐ _____

☐ _____

People I Love

Standard

Uses prewriting strategies to plan written work

Materials

- *Ida, Idea Creator* poster (page 64; ida.pdf)
- Chart paper
- Markers
- *People I Love* (page 82; peopleilove.pdf)

Mentor Texts

- *A Chair for My Mother* by Vera Williams
- *My Mom* by Anthony Browne
- *Just Me and My Mom* by Mercer Mayer
- *Just Me and My Dad* by Mercer Mayer
- *We Are Best Friends* by Aliki
- See *Mentor Text List* in Appendix C for other suggestions.

Procedures

Note: This lesson is especially appropriate to use as an end-of-year Author's Tea or Author's Luncheon activity. Invite family members, neighbors, and other teachers to hear their child's special tribute. Every child needs to be represented by someone. This lesson may be split into two days. On day one, develop a whole-class anchor chart and have students develop individual charts. On day two, have students develop ideas about one special person. Have students store their ideas in the green dot side of their writing folders.

Think About Writing

1. Tell students that each of them is surrounded by important people who influence the way they think and act. Sometimes these people are parents, sometimes siblings (brothers and sisters), and sometimes grandparents or even neighbors. In some situations, it is a teacher who influences their lives. These relationships with influential people blossom into stories that they can keep forever. Display the *Ida, Idea Creator* poster (page 64) and remind students that we are constantly seeking ways to refuel our idea tank.

2. Review a mentor text if desired, and emphasize the special people in our lives who can provide ideas for writing.

Teach

3. Tell students, "Today I will show you how to use the special people you have in your lives as a starting point for your stories." Use *People I Love* (page 82) to model how to create a list of important people. Think aloud about the people who are important to you as you record their names on the chart. The list might include your mom, dad, brothers, sisters, grandparents, and people in the community you admire. Write the list fairly quickly. Tell students you will keep this list of people handy so you can return to it when you need ideas for writing.

People I Love (cont.)

4. Select one person from the list and think of details about that special person. On a separate sheet of chart paper, write four details about the person and provide a wrap-up, or concluding sentence, which can loop back to the beginning statement and be rephrased. Be certain to model succinctly, talking and thinking aloud as you complete your writing text.

Engage

5. Have students *Turn and Talk* to partners and talk about people they know and care about that they want to remember. Provide approximately two minutes for partners to talk.

Apply

6. Ask students to remember how the special people in their lives are important to them as writers. Tell students those special people become seeds for stories so that they are never without ideas in Writer's Workshop. Tell students they will make their own *People I Love* lists.

Write/Conference

7. Distribute *People I Love* to students. Have students write for 5–10 minutes. As students work, rotate around the room having conversations with students about their lists. Remember to prod students to know the "why" and "how." This will help them in writing. Keep notes in your Conferring Notebook so that you will know whether to revisit this lesson or move ahead. Remember to offer students many compliments about work well done.

Spotlight Strategy

8. Spotlight a student who has an interesting *People I Love* list. "Special kudos to Julia for brilliant writing work! She created a list of special people that she can use in her writing."

Share

9. Have students meet with writing partners and share the names of the people on their lists.

Homework

Ask students to tell someone at home about the special people lists we are creating at school. Have them explain to their parents or caregivers that these lists offer ideas for stories we can write. Have students ask their parents for help thinking about other people from their lives they can add to their lists. Have students write a list of the names of at least five additional people they would like to write about.

Name: _____ **Date:** _____

People I Love

Directions: Make a list of the people that you love.

☐ _____

☐ _____

☐ _____

☐ _____

☐ _____

☐ _____

☐ _____

☐ _____

☐ _____

☐ _____

Sentence Fluency
Getting Started

Sentence fluency helps make writing interesting. It is a trait that allows writers to add a lot of depth to their writing. By changing sentence length and where words are placed next to each other in a sentence, writers are able to help guide the reader through their work. Authors with good sentence fluency know the techniques needed to construct sentences that flow and have rhythm. These lessons assist students in exploring parts of sentences, ways sentences are built, and techniques to expand sentences to develop more interesting ideas. Lessons in this section include the following:

- Lesson 1: Using Sentence Stems (page 85)
- Lesson 2: Popcorn Sentences (page 88)
- Lesson 3: Super Sentence Stems (page 90)
- Lesson 4: Building Sentences 1—Subjects (page 93)
- Lesson 5: Building Sentences 2—Predicates (page 101)
- Lesson 6: Building Sentences 3—Details (page 110)
- Lesson 7: Crawlin' Phrases (page 112)
- Lesson 8: The Sentence Game (page 116)
- Lesson 9: And Then… (page 122)
- Lesson 10: Writing Detectives: Sentences (pages 124)

The *Simon, Sentence Builder* poster (page 84) can be displayed in the room to provide a visual reminder for students that *Sentence Fluency* is one of the traits of writing. You may wish to introduce this poster during the first lesson on sentence fluency. Then, refer to the poster when teaching other lessons on sentence fluency to refresh students' memories and provide them with questions to help guide them as they create sentences.

Simon

Sentence Builder

What kinds of sentences will I use?

✔ Did I use long, medium, and short sentences?

✔ Did I use statements and questions?

✔ Did I use different sentence beginnings?

✔ Do my sentences flow smoothly when I read them aloud?

Using Sentence Stems

Standard

Uses strategies to draft and revise written work

Materials

- Chart paper
- Marker
- Sentence strips *(optional)*
- *Sample Sentence Stems* (page 87; samplesentencestems.pdf)

Mentor Texts

- *Brown Bear, Brown Bear* by Bill Martin, Jr.
- *Polar Bear, Polar Bear* by Bill Martin, Jr.
- *The Very Hungry Caterpillar* by Eric Carle
- *I Went Walking* by Sue Williams
- See *Mentor Text List* in Appendix C for other suggestions.

Procedures

Note: Consider using the sentence stems: *I can… Mom can…* or *Dad can…* This eliminates pressure on children because these words are known words and are easy to spell correctly. Repeat this lesson several times using different sentence starters. Gradually introduce other sentence stems.

Think About Writing

1. Explain that some authors stretch out their stories over several pages by using the same sentence starter.

2. Review a mentor text. Have students help identify the sentence pattern. Tell students that these stories help us learn to read. We can also use this same structure to help us write.

Teach

3. Tell students, "Today I will show you how to use a patterned structure to improve your writing stamina and create interesting stories." Tell students sentence stems can give them ideas for their writing. Select several sentence stems of your own or from *Sample Sentence Stems* (page 87) and write them on sentence strips.

4. Model for students how to choose a sentence stem and use it to write several sentences. Use the stems to make a pattern with the sentences you write. Write the sentences on chart paper for students to see. As you write, think aloud so students can understand your thought process when writing with sentence stems. In the modeling phase, phonetically spell words you have not introduced in classroom instruction. The goal is to increase the quantity of writing, constantly raising expectations. For example:

   My mom can cook our dinner. *My dad can* fix my toy. *My mom can* make our bed. *My dad can* tie my shoes. *My mom and dad can* help me.

   Notice the changed pattern in the last line. This models and creates the expectation of sentence variety.

Using Sentence Stems (cont.)

Engage

5. Have students *Heads-up, Stand-up, Partner-up* and work with partners to orally create a few interesting sentences using the sentence stems that are displayed. Remind students to take turns. Encourage students to give compliments and praise.

Apply

6. Remind students that sometimes authors use sentence patterns to share their stories. Encourage students to use the sentence stems that are displayed in the classroom. You may wish to provide specific paper or folded paper for a book.

Write/Conference

7. Provide time for students to write. When students are involved in their writing, begin to confer with individuals or small groups. Make certain the student you are conferring with is doing the major proportion of talking. End the conference by stating what the student should do next.

Spotlight Strategy

8. Spotlight a student who has done a great job using sentence stems. For example, "How exciting! Notice how Rahul has used sentence stems from the chart as an idea and has crafted brilliant sentences to weave into a story. You're right on target!"

Share

9. Tell students you will choose someone to sit in the Author's Chair. Remind students to be excellent listeners and ready to pay a compliment or ask a question. Provide approximately three minutes for a student to share.

Homework

Ask students to think of all the sentence stems they can use for writing stories and books. Ask them to create a list of at least five of their own sentence stems. For example: I can…, I will…, My mom…, My dad…, My favorite…., On Monday…. Ask them to be ready to share their lists in Writer's Workshop tomorrow.

Sample Sentence Stems

I like...	I do not like...
My mom...	My dad...
I can...	I cannot...
The dog...	The cat...
The car...	The truck...
The boy...	The girl...

Popcorn Sentences

Standard

Uses strategies to draft and revise written work

Materials

- *Sample Sentence Stems* (page 87; samplesentencestems.pdf)

Mentor Texts

- *A Chair for My Mother* by Vera B. Williams
- See *Mentor Text List* in Appendix C for other suggestions.

Procedures

Note: This lesson is crucial for helping students develop their writing through talking. It supports current research on helping children who come from environments with restricted speech. It can be repeated several times throughout the year to reinforce the idea of expanding sentences.

Think About Writing

1. Tell students that one of the greatest tools for learning is reading the work of other authors. Explain that we can study and explore how authors use words and sentences that flow together to tell a story.

2. Review the mentor text if desired, and emphasize the author's use of different sentence lengths. Read several sentences from the book and discuss their length.

Teach

3. Tell students, "Today I will show you how to build your sentence length in oral language and written language." Have students hold up one finger at a time to count the number of letters you say as you spell the word *popcorn*. Discuss how many letters there are in the word (seven).

4. Tell students they will make *popcorn sentences* by working with a partner to create sentences that have the same number of words (seven). Explain that partner one will say a sentence and partner two will count the number of words in the sentence. Demonstrate how to use your fingers to count the number of words you say in a sentence. Tell partners the goal is to create sentences that have seven words or more.

5. Model with a student partner how to be the sentence creator and the sentence counter. Remind students to use their ears to help them hear how words are connected to create smooth, fluent sentences. Encourage students to celebrate their partner's sentences.

Popcorn Sentences (cont.)

Engage

6. Have students *Heads-up, Stand-up, Partner-up* and practice orally creating sentences with their partners. You may wish to provide some sentence stems such as: *Today I am…, My mom…, That silly dog…, Last night…,* etc. You may also distribute *Sample Sentence Stems* (page 87).

Apply

7. Tell students that writers think and play with words in sentences. Encourage them to use their ears as tools to hear both long and short sentences in their writing.

Write/Conference

8. Provide time for students to write. Once students are settled, begin conferring with individuals or small groups of students. Remember to use your Conferring Notebook to keep notes.

Spotlight Strategy

9. Spotlight a sentence with seven or more words. For example, "Listen to this marvelous sentence. Hannah used sentences just like the authors whose book we read. Smart writing work!"

Share

10. Move students into triads, and have them pick out their best sentence to share. Provide approximately two minutes to share.

Homework

Ask students to teach a sibling, parent, or someone else at home how to be a sentence creator and a sentence counter. Have students practice so each person plays both roles.

Super Sentence Stems

Procedures

Note: Repetitive phrases and sentences support students as they begin to add quantity to their writing.

Think About Writing

1. Explain that sometimes authors use sentence or phrase patterns to capture a reader's attention.

2. Review a mentor text if desired, and emphasize the repetitive phrases. For example, Margaret Wise Brown, in her book *The Runaway Bunny*, uses the phrases, "If you …, I will…" Tell students that she also adds interesting details to her phrase patterns.

Teach

3. Tell students, "Today I will show you how to use a sentence stem from our chart and link a couple of ideas together." Explain that you will begin with a sentence stem, and then strengthen the sentence so it is more interesting. Display *Sentence Builders* (page 92) for students and tell them they will each get a copy to put in their writing folders. Tell them they might also want to keep their own lists of interesting sentence stems or phrases.

4. Model how to use a sentence stem from *Sentence Builders* to begin a sentence. Write your sentence on a sheet of chart paper. Link a couple of ideas together to extend your writing. For example, "*I like* to go shopping with Mom at the store. I push the shopping cart and she fills it up. Shopping with Mom is fun!"

5. Draw students' attention to how you combined several ideas and extended a simple, "I like…" sentence stem to expand the idea of shopping at the store. Encourage students to study the sentence stems and find stems that are most appealing to them.

Super Sentence Stems *(cont.)*

Engage

6. Have students *Heads-up, Stand-up, Partner-up* and work with partners to orally practice using one of the sentence stems. Encourage students to connect three or more thoughts together. Have them use their fingers to count the ideas. Remind students that if they selected the sentence stem, *My mom...*, they should stick to that topic. Encourage them to add phrases that tell where, when, or how. Provide approximately three minutes for partners to practice.

Apply

7. Encourage students to practice making their stories longer by using sentence stems and phrases to develop super sentences. Remind students that when they talked with their partners, they linked their ideas. Encourage them to do the same in their writing.

Write/Conference

8. Provide time for students to write super sentences of their own. As students write, reteach to a small group or provide enrichment for those students ready to go beyond your expectations. Remember to keep notes in your Conferring Notebook.

Spotlight Strategy

9. Spotlight a great sentence writer. For example, "Awesome! Great planning! Christopher is a super sentence stretcher. Writers, you rock!"

Share

10. Have students work with partners to share their super sentences. Provide approximately two minutes for sharing.

Homework

Ask students to write one super sentence. Ask students to be ready to share their sentences with the class tomorrow.

Name: _____ Date: _____

Sentence Builders

I like...	My sister...	The boy...
I do not like...	My family...	That girl...
I like to eat...	My family likes to...	I see...
I don't like to eat...	The dog...	I saw...
I am...	A bird...	I went...
I can...	That cat...	I am thankful...
I cannot...	I have...	I know how to...
My friend...	I think...	I like to play...
My mom...	I love...	I go...
My dad...	My favorite...	If I were a...
My brother...	We go...	Can you...?

#50915—Core of Writing—Level 1

Building Sentences 1—Subjects

Standards

- Uses strategies to draft and revise written work
- Uses complete sentences in written compositions

Materials

- Chart paper
- Marker
- *Subject Cards* (pages 95–100; subjectcards.pdf)

Mentor Texts

- *Chrysanthemum* by Kevin Henkes
- See *Mentor Text List* in Appendix C for other suggestions.

Procedures

Note: This lesson focuses on the subject (or naming part) of a sentence.

Think About Writing

1. Tell students that smart writers work with their sentences and rewrite them to get just the right meaning to express interesting ideas in a clear, logical way. Sentences have two basic parts: a *subject* (the naming part) and a *predicate* (the action part).

Teach

2. Tell students, "Today I will show you how to put the two basic parts of a sentence together to capture just the right idea." Explain that sentences have two basic parts: a *subject*, or naming part, and a *predicate*, or action part.

3. Display *Subject Cards* (pages 95–100) one at a time. For each card, ask students: "Does it have a *subject* or naming part?" *(Yes)* "Does it have a *predicate* or action part?" *(No)* Remind students that sentences have a naming part *and* an action part.

4. Model for students how to create a sentence using the *Subject Cards*. Choose one *Subject Card* and generate your own predicate. Write the sentence on chart paper, thinking aloud as you write to remind students of correct punctuation, spacing, etc. Review the sentence with students. You may wish to use different colored markers to show the two parts of the sentence.

5. Create several more sentences as needed.

Building Sentences 1—Subjects *(cont.)*

Engage

6. Have students *Turn and Talk* with partners to orally create sentences. Display a *Subject Card* and have students complete the sentence with an action part. Ask students to listen carefully to their partner's sentences to consider if the sentence makes sense. Provide enough opportunities for students to practice creating the action parts.

Apply

7. Tell students that they will be writing sentences, starting with the naming part, or *subject*. Remind students to always be thinking about their sentences to see if they are reasonable and make sense. Encourage them to repeat their sentences in their heads to check for meaning and sentence fluency. Tell students they may use the *Subject Cards* or think of their own naming parts. Display the *Subject Cards* for the whole class or allow students to work in quads and place a few cards at each table.

Write/Conference

8. Provide time for students to write. Once students are settled, begin conferring with individuals or small groups of students. Remember to use your Conferring Notebook to keep notes to assist in making instructional decisions.

Spotlight Strategy

9. Spotlight a great sentence writer. For example, "Amazing sentence work! Listen to the sentence that Melinda has created. You are such smart writers. Keep up this astonishing work."

Share

10. Have students create quads and share two of their best sentences with the group. Provide three minutes for students to share their work. Remind students to compliment and ask questions about each other's work.

Homework

Ask students to write one sentence that links a naming word and an action together to make a sentence.

Subject Cards

Teacher Directions: Cut out the cards below and display them for students. Then, model how to create a sentence using at least one *Subject Card*.

 **The boy**

 **His mom**

 **Her dad**

 **That girl**

Subject Cards (cont.)

 **The baby**

 **My brother**

 **His grandpa**

 **My teacher**

Subject Cards (cont.)

 **A queen**

 **That clown**

 **The fireman**

 **A policewoman**

Subject Cards (cont.)

 **The tiger**

 **A monkey**

 **The zebra**

 **A snake**

Subject Cards (cont.)

 **A cat**

 **That spider**

 **A puppy**

 **A frog**

Subject Cards (cont.)

 **My present**

 **A snowflake**

 **The snowman**

 **This tree**

Building Sentences 2—Predicates

Procedures

Note: This lesson focuses on the *predicate* (or action part) of a sentence.

Think About Writing

1. Remind students that a sentence has to have a *subject*, or naming part, and a *predicate*, or action part. Tell students that authors are careful to write sentences that make sense to their readers.

2. Review a mentor text if desired, and emphasize the subjects and predicates in several sentences.

Teach

3. Tell students, "Today I will show you how to use the two basic parts of a sentence to capture just the right idea." Display the *Predicate Cards* (pages 103–109), one at a time. For each card, ask students: "Does it have a *subject* or naming part?" *(No)* "Does it have a *predicate* or action part?" *(Yes)* Remind students that sentences have a naming part *and* an action part.

4. Model for students how to create a sentence using the *Predicate Cards*. Choose one *Predicate Card* and generate your own subject. Write the sentence on chart paper, thinking aloud as you write to remind students of correct punctuation, spacing, etc. Review the sentence with students. You may wish to use different colored markers to show the two parts of the sentence.

5. Create several more sentences as needed.

Building Sentences 2—Predicates *(cont.)*

Engage

6. Have students *Heads-up, Stand-up, Partner-up* and work with partners to orally create sentences. Display a *Predicate Card* and have students complete the sentence with a subject. Ask students to listen carefully to their partner's sentences to consider if the sentence makes sense. Provide enough opportunities for students to practice creating the subjects.

Apply

7. Tell students that they will be writing sentences based on an action part, or *predicate*. Remind students to always be thinking about their sentences to see if they are reasonable and make sense. Encourage them to repeat their sentences in their heads to check for meaning and sentence fluency. Tell students they may use the *Predicate Cards* or think of their own action parts. Display the *Predicate Cards* for the whole class or allow students to work in quads and place a few cards at each table.

Write/Conference

8. Provide time for students to write sentences based on the cards. Once students are settled, begin conferring with individuals or small groups of students. Remember to use your Conferring Notebook to keep notes to assist in making instructional decisions.

Spotlight Strategy

9. Spotlight a student who has written an outstanding sentence. For example, "Tina has written an outstanding sentence. You are such brilliant writers. Keep up this amazing work."

Share

10. Have students create quads and share two of their best sentences with the group. Provide three minutes for students to share their work. Remind students to compliment and ask questions about each other's work.

Homework

Ask students to write one sentence each that links a naming part and action part.

Predicate Cards

Teacher Directions: Cut out the cards below and display them for students. Then, model how to create a sentence using at least one *Predicate Card*.

plays football.

jumps on the bed.

drives a truck.

plays with the bear.

Predicate Cards (cont.)

bakes cookies.

likes to read.

takes a bath.

kisses a frog.

Predicate Cards (cont.)

puts out the fire.

flies to the moon.

has a funny hat.

chases the mouse.

Predicate Cards (cont.)

chews on a bone.

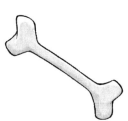

eats flies.

has eight legs.

lives at the zoo.

Predicate Cards (cont.)

swings in the trees.

likes to fish.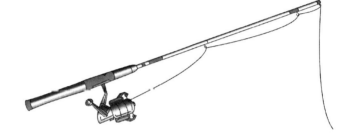

slides through the grass.

has sharp teeth.

Predicate Cards (cont.)

has a big nose.

likes toys.

likes milk and cookies.

wears a blue scarf.

#50915—Core of Writing—Level 1

Predicate Cards (cont.)

can run very fast.

is under the tree.

lands on my shoulder.

has many leaves.

Building Sentences 3—Details

Procedures

Note: The focus of this mini-lesson is on adding details to a sentence.

Think About Writing

1. Review with students that sentences have subjects, or naming parts, and predicates, or action parts. Remind students that they are also being careful that their sentences make sense, like real writers do.

2. Review a mentor text if desired, and emphasize the author's use of sentences with varying lengths. For example, writers like Kevin Henkes make sure they have some short sentences and some long sentences in their stories. Changing the length of the sentences helps keep readers interested and the stories fun to read.

Teach

3. Tell students, "Today I will show you how to add detail to your sentences to make them longer and more interesting."

4. Model for students how to choose a *Subject Card* (pages 95–100) and a *Predicate Card* (pages 103–109) to create a sentence. The sentence can be silly or serious. Write the sentence on chart paper. For example, *The puppy jumps on the bed.*

5. Expand the sentence by adding a detail. Use the dice or spinner to determine what detail to add to your writing. For example, if the spinner lands on *when*, the sentence could be expanded to read, "The puppy jumps on the bed every morning." Use different colored markers to demonstrate the different parts of the sentence.

Standards

- Uses strategies to draft and revise written work
- Uses complete sentences in written compositions

Materials

- Chart paper
- Markers
- *Subject Cards* (pages 95–100; subjectcards.pdf)
- *Predicate Cards* (pages 103–109; predicatecards.pdf)
- Dice or spinner with 5 W questions: Who? What? Where? When? Why?

Mentor Texts

- *Chrysanthemum* by Kevin Henkes
- See *Mentor Text List* in Appendix C for other suggestions.

Building Sentences 3—Details (cont.)

Engage

6. Have students *Heads-up, Stand-up, Partner-up* and work in pairs to orally create sentences using the subject and predicate cards, and adding details. Provide enough opportunities for students to practice creating and adding details to sentences.

Apply

7. Tell students that they will be writing sentences with a subject and predicate and adding details. Remind students to always be thinking about their sentences to see if they have a subject, a predicate, and some details. Encourage students to repeat their sentences in their heads to check for meaning and sentence fluency. Determine if you want students to work independently or with partners based on writing development.

Write/Conference

8. Provide time for students to write. Scan your class for understanding of the sentence strategy; then, begin to confer with individuals or small groups of students. Remember to keep anecdotal observations to assist in making instructional decisions.

Spotlight Strategy

9. Spotlight a student with excellent details in their sentence. For example, "Fabulous sentence work! Listen to the details in the sentence that Gabrielle has created. You are such smart writers. **WOW**! **W**hat **O**utstanding **W**riters!"

Share

10. Have students share their new sentences in quads. Provide approximately three minutes for students to share their best work. Remind students to give compliments. You may wish for everyone to edit and illustrate their work and then do a class share for display.

Homework

Ask students to write one sentence that links words and phrases with naming parts and action parts to make sentences that will excite readers.

Crawlin' Phrases

Standard

Uses strategies to draft and revise written work

Materials

- Chart paper
- Marker
- Apples
- Chenille stem "worms" or gummy worms
- *Crawlin' Preposition Phrases* (page 114; crawlinprepphrases.pdf)
- *Prepositions* (page 115; prepositions.pdf)
- Large sticky notes

Mentor Texts

- *The Relatives Came* by Cynthia Rylant
- *We're Going on a Bear Hunt* by Helen Oxenbury and Michael Rosen
- *Over, Under and Through* by Tana Hoban
- See *Mentor Text List* in Appendix C for other suggestions.

Procedures

Note: Some first-grade students have not yet mastered the directional words needed to effectively write prepositional phrases. Monitor students to determine who may need additional instruction individually or in a small group setting.

Think About Writing

1. Tell students that writers build and shape sentences by adding details to their writing. This helps the readers see the story in their minds.

2. Review a mentor text if desired, and emphasize the author's use of phrases. For example, explain that writers like Cynthia Rylant add phrases to give their readers more information. In *The Relatives Came,* instead of writing, "We waved goodbye," she wrote, "We stood there in our pajamas and waved them off in the dark." Tell students this really helps the reader picture them standing in the early morning darkness, still in their pajamas.

Teach

3. Tell students, "Today I will show you how to use prepositional phrases to add sentence variety and details to your writing." Explain that a prepositional phrase usually shows the reader where or when something occurred. Share other passages from a mentor text. Work with students to identify prepositional phrases. You may wish to create a chart of phrases that the class finds.

4. Write the sentence *The worm crawls _____ the apple.* on a sheet of chart paper. Use an apple and worm to demonstrate a place where the worm can go. For example, "The worm crawls *under* the apple." Write the word *under* on a sticky note and put it in the blank on the sentence. Read the sentence aloud. Repeat several times as needed.

Crawlin' Phrases (cont.)

Engage

5. Tell students they will work in groups to create their own worm sentences. Divide students into triads or quads. Provide each group of students with copies of *Crawlin' Preposition Phrases* (page 114). Display the *Prepositions* poster (page 115) or provide one to each group. Tell students to create sentences to show where the worm can be on the apple. Provide approximately five to seven minutes for groups to work.

6. Gather students back together and discuss the prepositions they used.

Apply

7. Tell students that they will write using prepositional phrases. Remind students that including prepositional phrases in their sentences will not only add variety in their sentence length but also add details to show the reader their writing.

Write/ Conference

8. Provide time for students to write on any topic. Scan to problem solve before moving off to confer. Ask questions, such as "What are you working on as a writer?" "How will this help you as a writer?" and "What do you plan to do next?"

Spotlight Strategy

9. Spotlight a student with fantastic ideas. For example, "Look at all your amazing ideas." Be sure to notice those students who generated prepositional phrases in their writing. Call attention to students who were quick in getting started on the task. Always notice and compliment strong work ethic.

Share

10. Provide approximately two minutes for students to share their ideas with partners. Based on your observations, choose one or two students who clearly understood prepositional phrases and have them share with the whole group.

Homework

Ask students to make a list of three other prepositional phrase ideas. For example: *at the table*, *in my bed*, and *across the street*. Tell students to be ready to share their lists tomorrow.

Name: _____ Date: _____

Crawlin' Preposition Phrases

Directions: Make sentences to show where the worm can be with the apple.

The worm crawls _____ the apple.

The worm crawls _____ the apple.

The worm crawls _____ the apple.

The worm crawls _____ the apple.

#50915—Core of Writing—Level 1

Prepositions

A *prepositional phrase* begins with a preposition and shows the reader where, when, or how something occurred.

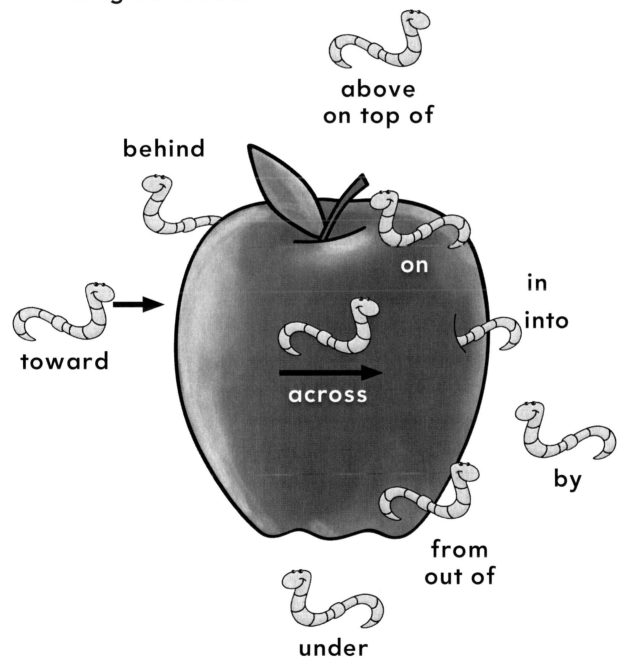

The worm crawls _____ the apple.

The Sentence Game

Standards

- Uses strategies to draft and revise written work
- Uses complete sentences in written compositions

Materials

- Chart paper
- Marker
- *Sentence Picture Cards* (pages 118–121; sentencepicturecards.pdf)
- Index cards

Mentor Texts

- *The Relatives Came* by Cynthia Rylant
- See *Mentor Text List* in Appendix C for other suggestions.

Procedures

Think About Writing

1. Tell students that the words and pictures need to match the message of a writing piece. Explain that many authors put words together so they seem to dance across the page to make musical sentences.

2. Review a mentor text if desired, and emphasize several interesting sentences the author wrote. Tell students, "Notice how Cynthia Rylant's words move across the page and have lots of details in *The Relatives Came*. For instance, she writes, 'We stood there *in our pajamas* and waved them off *in the dark*. We watched the relatives disappear *down the road*, then we crawled back *into our beds* that felt too big and too quiet.' The details in the sentence make the story easier to picture."

Teach

3. Tell students, "Today I will show you how to use what you have learned about subjects and predicates to write sentences. Then, we will add interesting details for our readers." Explain that in order to add details, we can begin asking questions like *when* and *where*.

4. Tell students *when* and *where* are such important questions that they are going to create question cards with those words. Distribute index cards. Have them write *when* on one side of the card and *where* on the other side. Tell students by answering these questions in their sentences, they will create great sentences.

5. Write *My cat* on a sheet of chart paper. Tell students that is the subject. Then write *sleeps all day*. Tell students that is the predicate. Explain that to add detail, we can add *on my bed* to the sentence. This tells the reader *where* the cat sleeps. Now the reader can see my cat curled up on my bed.

The Sentence Game (cont.)

6. Remind students of the structure a sentence can have:

Subject	Predicate	Detail/ Prepositional Phrase
My cat	sleeps all day	on my bed.
A spider	spins a web	in the corner.
My sister	made a cake	last night.

Use the *Sentence Picture Cards* (pages 118–121) to practice and write sentences on the chart .

Engage

7. Tell students they are going to play *The Sentence Game*. Have students work with their partners to create a sentence with a subject, a predicate, and a detail. Encourage students to use the question cards they created. Model how to play the game with a student partner prior to having students work with their partners. Practice with several picture cards as needed. Have students *Heads-up, Stand-up, Partner-up*.

Apply

8. Remind students that writing sentences using details helps the reader see their stories more clearly. Encourage students to write some sentences using this simple lesson.

Write/ Conference

9. Provide time for students to write. Check for understanding and rotate among students to confer and support. Note observations in your Conferring Notebook.

Spotlight Strategy

10. Spotlight a student who showed amazing sentence work. For example, "Look at all your brilliant sentences! Chani has a sentence that is simply dancing across the page with a subject, a predicate, and a detail. Smart writing work!"

Share

11. Have students share their writing work with a new partner. Provide approximately two minutes for students to share. Then, select a few students who demonstrated skill to share their work with the whole group.

Homework
Ask students to play *The Sentence Game* with their parents or sibling tonight.

Sentence Picture Cards

Teacher Directions: Cut out the cards below. Use the *Sentence Picture Cards* to practice writing sentences with students by forming sentences about the picture on each card. Be sure students include a subject, predicate, and prepositional phrase in their sentences.

Sentence Picture Cards (cont.)

Sentence Picture Cards (cont.)

Sentence Picture Cards (cont.)

And Then...

Standard

Uses strategies to draft and revise written work

Materials

- Highlighting tape
- Chart paper
- Markers

Mentor Texts

- *Chrysanthemum* by Kevin Henkes
- See *Mentor Text List* in Appendix C for other suggestions.

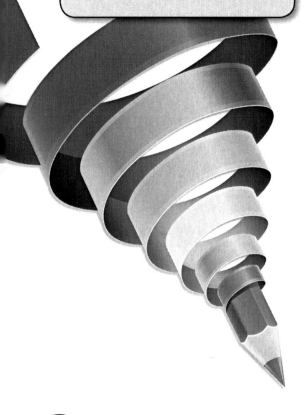

Procedures

Note: This mini-lesson may be implemented over several days and revisited each month.

Think About Writing

1. Remind students that building interesting sentences shows our thoughts to our readers. Good writers use a variety of sentences to create interest and excitement. Unless we are writing a special pattern book, it is important to begin our sentences in different ways.

2. Review a mentor text if desired, and emphasize the author's use of interesting sentences.

Teach

3. Tell students, "Today I will show you how to identify different ways you can begin your sentences."

4. Display a big book that has sentences with a variety of sentences and not a patterned text. Use highlighting tape to highlight the first word in four or five sentences. Point out to students how the author of the book begins his or her sentences. Chart the first word or words of several sentences for students to compare.

5. Tell students they will work with partners to find examples of a variety of sentence beginnings.

Engage

6. Have students *Heads-up, Stand-up, Partner-up* and work with partners to look through some books to find examples of sentence beginning variety. Gather students back together. Provide time for students to share with the whole class what they discovered.

And Then... *(cont.)*

Apply

7. Remind students to be aware of how they begin sentences as they write. Encourage them to concentrate on using a variety of beginnings. Suggest that students make lists of the first two words in sentences they write. They can keep this list in their writing folders.

Write/Conference

8. Provide time for students to write. Observe student behaviors. Are they on task? Controlled? Regulated? Then, begin having conversations with students and making notes about writing behaviors.

Spotlight Strategy

9. Spotlight a student with great sentence variety. For example, "Marcia is checking over her sentence beginnings and is making revisions to improve her story." Encourage the whole class to celebrate by having them *Stop, Stand, and Celebrate.* Have students stop what they are doing, stand up, and celebrate by waving their hands over their heads.

Share

10. Ask students to lock eyes with someone with whom they would like to have a conversation. Ask them to partner up and share their collected sentence variety and how they applied this in their writing.

Homework

Ask students to explore different types of writing like books, newspapers, and magazines, and look for sentence beginnings. Ask students to make a list of five different ways the print material they looked at begins. Tell them to be ready to share what they noticed tomorrow.

Writing Detective: Sentences

Standards

- Uses strategies to draft and revise written work
- Uses complete sentences in written compositions

Materials

- Chart paper
- Markers
- *Writing Detective Cards* (page 126; writingdetectivecards.pdf)
- *Be a Writing Detective* (page 127; bewritingdetective.pdf)

Mentor Texts

- *Chrysanthemum* by Kevin Henkes
- See *Mentor Text List* in Appendix C for other suggestions.

Procedures

Note: The process used in this lesson about sentences can also be used to add details to a paragraph.

Think About Writing

1. Remind students that sentences have a subject and predicate. They have also been learning to select just the right words. Good writers know that details are important and make writing so much more interesting for their readers.

2. Review a mentor text if desired, and emphasize the author's use of interesting sentences.

Teach

3. Tell students, "Today I will show you how to use questions to add details to build your sentences." Explain to students that they will be writing detectives asking the following questions: Wh*o?*, *What?*, *When?*, *Where?*, and *Why?*

4. Write the sentence *My cat bites me!* on a sheet of chart paper. Tell students that sentence does not give readers much information.

5. Display the *Writing Detective Cards* (page 126) to students. Think aloud as you develop your sentence. For example, "*Who* will be in my sentence? Roxy, my cat. *What* is happening? She bites my toes!" Then, pick one question word from the *Writing Detective Card*—where. *Where* does it happen? On my bed. So, my sentence will be *My cat Roxy jumps on my bed and bites my toes.*

   Tell students you like that sentence much better. It gives the reader a much stronger mental picture of the writing.

Writing Detective: Sentences (cont.)

Engage

6. Tell students to *Heads-up, Stand-up, Partner-up* and work with partners to be writing detectives. Provide students with *Writing Detective Cards*. Provide students two or three minutes to create sentences that have a subject and predicate, and answer a question from the card. Ask a few partner pairs to share their sentences.

Apply

7. Remind students to give their readers writing details to invite them into their writing. Tell students that the *Writing Detective Card* can be a valuable tool as they write. Remind them to keep it in their writing folders so it will be handy while they are writing.

Write/Conference

8. Provide time for students to write their own sentences. Scan the class for understanding of the sentence strategy. Meet with students having difficulty with sentence structure and use this strategy to support their efforts. You may wish to help struggling students use *Be a Writing Detective* (page 127) to guide their sentence writing efforts. Record compliments and teaching points in your Conferring Notebook.

Spotlight Strategy

9. Spotlight a student who used question words well to add detail. For example, "Listen to the sentence Elian has created while being a writing detective. I am so proud of his exceptional work. Spotlight on Elian!"

Share

10. Have students meet with partners to share their work. Encourage students to ask their partners which questions were used to develop the sentences they shared.

Homework

Ask students to look around and find ideas for creating great sentences. Tell them to create three sentences at home and add them to their folder during Writer's Workshop tomorrow.

Writing Detective Cards

Teacher Directions: Create copies of this sheet. Cut out the cards and distribute them to students. Have students use two questions on the cards to expand their sentences.

Be a Writing Detective!	**Be a Writing Detective!**
Who?	**Who?**
What?	**What?**
When?	**When?**
Where?	**Where?**
Why?	**Why?**

#50915—Core of Writing—Level 1   © *Shell Education*

Name: _____ Date: _____

Be a Writing Detective

Directions: Think about the questions below. Choose a subject and a predicate. Then, write a sentence that answers one of the questions.

- **Who?**

- **What?**

- **When?**

- **Where?**

- **Why?**

My Sentence:

_____

_____

_____

_____

Organization
Linking the Pieces Together

Organization provides the structure of writing. It helps readers make connections from one idea to the next. Organization provides the skeletal support for the overall meaning of writing. These lessons assist students in exploring different types of writing and the ways they are organized. Lessons in this section include the following:

- Lesson 1: Matching Text to Picture (page 131)
- Lesson 2: Making Alphabet Books (page 134)
- Lesson 3: My First Book (page 136)
- Lesson 4: Hand Plan (page 138)
- Lesson 5: Telling, Sketching, and Writing Informative Text (page 143)
- Lesson 6: Telling, Sketching, and Writing Narrative Text (page 145)
- Lesson 7: Using Speech Bubbles (page 148)
- Lesson 8: Writing a Letter (page 150)
- Lesson 9: Addressing an Envelope (page 153)
- Lesson 10: I Know How To… (page 155)
- Lesson 11: Poetry: Simple Acrostic (page 158)
- Lesson 12: Poetry: Five Ws Poem (page 160)

The *Owen, Organization Conductor* poster (page 130) can be displayed in the room to provide a visual reminder for students that Organization is one of the traits of writing. You may choose to introduce this poster during the first lesson on organization, and refer to it when teaching other organization lessons as review.

Owen
Organization
Conductor

How do I plan my writing?

✔ Did I sequence my thoughts?

✔ Did I have a beginning, middle, and end?

✔ Did I hook my reader?

✔ Did I include transition words?

Matching Text to Picture

Standard

Uses strategies to organize written work

Materials

- Chart paper
- Marker
- Green dot stickers or a green marker
- *My Picture Checklist* (page 133; picchecklist.pdf)
- 8.5" × 11" paper

Mentor Texts

- *Mrs. Wishy-Washy's Farm* by Joy Cowley
- Any familiar picture book with appropriate text/picture match
- See *Mentor Text List* in Appendix C for other suggestions.

Procedures

Note: You may wish to create an anchor chart to display in the classroom with the items from the picture checklist.

Think About Writing

1. Tell students that there are many different ways to tell our thoughts. Sometimes, good writers use pictures to support the message and the image they hope to leave in the reader's mind.

2. On a sheet of chart paper, write the sentence: *The sun's rays squeezed through the crack in the old wooden fence.* Explain to students that you would want a picture showing the sun in the background with old brown cracked boards and the sun's rays shining through. Reinforce the idea that pictures help readers understand and decode tricky words in an author's message. Review the mentor text if desired, and emphasize that the pictures match the details.

Teach

3. Tell students, "Today I will show you how to match the text you have written to a picture that supports your message." Fold a sheet of 8.5" × 11" paper in half so it opens top to bottom (so they have more space to write). Unfold the paper and place a green sticker dot at the top half in the left-hand corner.

4. Model how to think of an idea for writing. Think aloud so students are provided with specific examples of how you choose your topic. For example, "I can write about the things I know most about, like my family or things I like to do. Today, I am going to write a story about my son. My son likes to play football, so I think I'll write about that." Point out the green dot sticker where you will start writing. Model writing the sentence beginning at the green dot. Use spelling that is appropriate to the developmental level of your students.

Matching Text to Picture *(cont.)*

5. Distribute *My Picture Checklist* (page 133) to students. Tell students this checklist helps them remember to include things in their picture that will help support the sentence. Think aloud as you draw your picture on the bottom half of the folded paper and check off the items on the checklist. It is important for students to clearly see you making attempts at sketching. This will encourage them to become risk-takers in their own writing and sketching. As writers develop, add additional details to pictures that can be reflected in sentences. Your modeling prompts mimicking; if you write two thoughts, the students will also.

Engage

6. Ask students to think of an idea that they will use in a story. Have them *Turn and Talk* to partners and clearly articulate what they will write and what illustrations they will use to help tell the story. Provide approximately three minutes.

Apply

7. Give students paper and green dot stickers, and show them how to fold the paper and place the green dot. Tell students they will write on the half with the green dot and draw their picture on the other half. Remind students to make their pictures and words match so that the reader can understand their messages.

Write/Conference

8. Provide time for students to write sentences and draw. Scan your group to be certain everyone understands; if students are not clear about your intention, then gather a small group and reteach quickly. Then begin meeting with students to have conversations about their writing.

Spotlight Strategy

9. Spotlight a student who does a great job matching words to pictures. For example, "Wow! What smart writers! Vivica has an excellent picture that helps the reader visualize exactly what is happening in the text. Amazing, important writing work today."

Share

10. Have students meet in pairs to share their writing. Ask students to check if their partner's pictures and words match.

Homework

Ask students to draw a picture and write one sentence that matches the picture.

Name: _____ Date: _____

My Picture Checklist

Directions: Use the checklist below to help you draw your picture. Make sure you include all parts of the checklist in the picture to support your story.

☐ **Characters:** Who is in the story?

☐ **Setting:** Where and when does the story take place?

☐ **Words or Sentences:** Tell about my picture.

☐ **Picture:** My picture tells a story.

Making Alphabet Books

Standards

- Uses strategies to organize written work
- Writes in a variety of forms or genres

Materials

- Drawing paper
- *My Alphabet Book* (abcbook.pdf)

Mentor Texts

- *Jambo Means Hello: Swahili African Alphabet* by Muriel Feelings
- See *Mentor Text List* in Appendix C for other suggestions.

Procedures

Note: You may wish to create a class alphabet book to model the organization and format of an alphabet book. Also, this lesson can be used for all levels and with topics in all content areas, for example: weather, space, holidays, or community helpers. You may wish to have your letters already typed on the sheets of paper you distribute or have students write the letters themselves.

Think About Writing

1. Tell students there are many ways to organize books. Review with students the various ways they have already practiced. Tell students that writers constantly explore and experiment with many ways to write.

2. Review a mentor text if desired, and emphasize the book's organization around the alphabet.

Teach

3. Tell students, "Today I will show you how to organize a book around the alphabet." Review with students that the alphabet has 26 letters, so they will need to account for that as they plan how many pages to use. Tell students that some letters can share pages. For example, *Y* could be the top of the page and *Z* could be the bottom of the page.

4. Model how to create a page of an alphabet book. Choose a letter of the alphabet and write the uppercase and lowercase letter in the corner of the page. Draw a picture or pictures that begin with the letter. Label or write sentences to match the picture(s).

5. Tell students that alphabet books can be based on a topic or theme. For example, students could create an alphabet book about community helpers, animals, or their favorite storybook characters that begin with the beginning sound of each letter. Share examples of alphabet mentor texts on specific topics.

Making Alphabet Books (cont.)

Engage

6. Have students *Heads-up, Stand-up, Partner-up*. Assign each partner group a letter of the alphabet. Have partners think of as many words as they can that begin with their assigned letters.

Apply

7. Tell students that they can create their own alphabet books during Writer's Workshop. Explain that this is just one of many forms of writing the class will look at this year. Distribute *My Alphabet Book* (abcbook.pdf) to students.

Write/Conference

8. Provide time for students to work on their pages. Observe your class briefly for any uncertainties and reteach if necessary. When students are engaged, begin to compliment and teach individuals or small groups. Remember to keep records of your observations.

Spotlight Strategy

9. Spotlight a student with a great start to his or her alphabet book. For example, "What a brilliant beginning! Each of you is busy with your part of the alphabet book. Travis is working on the letter *T* and has an excellent drawing. His letters are perfectly formed and he is busy exploring ideas."

Share

10. Have students meet in triads to share their writing. Remind students to give a compliment and ask a question.

Homework

Ask students to play the game *I Spy*. Have them look for letters or objects that begin with each letter of the alphabet with friends or family members. Challenge them to go all the way through the alphabet from *A* to *Z*.

My First Book

Standard

Writes in a variety of forms or genres

Materials

- 8.5" × 11" paper
- Stapler
- *Subject Cards* (pages 95–100; subjectcards.pdf)

Mentor Texts

- *Wishy-Washy Day* by Joy Cowley
- See *Mentor Text List* in Appendix C for other suggestions.

Procedures

Note: You may wish to provide students with books that are already assembled or provide them with the paper and materials and show them how to assemble their own books. This lesson can be used with all text types and purposes: opinion, informative, or narrative.

Think About Writing

1. Tell students they will continue to practice writing words to match their pictures. Remind students they have been practicing beginning sentences with uppercase letters and ending them with a period.

2. Review a mentor text with students if desired, and emphasize the author's topic.

Teach

3. Tell students, "Today I will show you how to make your own books." Explain that they will need to decide what the books will be about. This is called the *idea* or *topic* for writing.

4. Tell students you have some pictures to help them with their ideas for writing. Select a picture to write about and talk about what you know about that picture. For example, the topic could be birds. Tell students that you know that birds fly, build nests, and eat worms.

5. Demonstrate how to fold a sheet of paper to make a little booklet. Fold two to three sheets of paper in half and staple the pages to make a book. Students can orient the book in either direction; however, at the beginning of the year, it is easier for them to write horizontally across the page with the book opening upward.

My First Book (cont.)

6. Model how to create the book. Think aloud as you model so students are provided with a concrete description of what you are doing. For example, "I will put the title of my book and my name just like Joy Cowley did in her book, *Wishy-Washy Day*." Now, I will open to my first page and write my first idea." Continue to model writing the text of the book. Think aloud through print concepts and spelling, and ensure that each of the ideas is related to the topic.

Engage

7. Display the *Subject Cards* (pages 95–100). Ask students to look at each picture and *Turn and Talk* with partners about any ideas they may have for writing topics. Provide approximately two minutes for students to share ideas after each picture. Listen in on conversations and share what you observed with children. Provide additional practice as time allows or students' needs dictate.

8. Have students decide on a topic to write about today. Ask them to turn to partners and share the topic they have chosen for their books. Encourage them to share one or two sentences about their ideas.

Apply

9. Ask students to think about their topic and ideas for sentences to go along with the topic. Provide each student with writing paper or an assembled book. Remind students to write the title and author's name on the front of the book before they begin writing inside.

Write/Conference

10. Provide time for students to write. Scan the class for understanding of book writing. Then, rotate among students and begin to confer with individuals or small groups of students.

Spotlight Strategy

11. Spotlight a student who has done a great job starting his or her book. For example, "Amazing book work! Listen to the sentence that Timothy has created about his idea."

Share

12. Have students meet with partners to share their stories. Remind students to offer compliments!

Homework

Ask students to talk with someone about the fabulous books they are writing in Writer's Workshop. Encourage students to think of new ideas for more book writing.

Hand Plan

Standard
Uses strategies to organize written work

Materials
- Chart paper
- Markers
- *My Hand Plan* (page 141; myhandplan.pdf)
- *Hand Plan Sample* (page 140; handplansample.pdf)
- *Topic Ideas* (page 142; topicideas.pdf)

Mentor Texts
- *The Sun Is My Favorite Star* by Frank Asch
- *Seeds* by Ken Robbins
- *Should We Have Pets?* by Sylvia Lollis
- *I Wanna New Room* by Karen Kaufmann Orloff
- *The Relatives Came* by Cynthia Rylant
- *Chrysanthemum* by Kevin Henkes
- *Peter's Chair* by Ezra Jack Keats
- See *Mentor Text List* in Appendix C for other suggestions.

Procedures
Note: This organizer may be used for all narrative, informative, and opinion paragraphs. Repeat this lesson throughout the year, modeling different genres each time. By the end of approximately 18 weeks of school, students should be able to write a complete paragraph. Remember to allow many opportunities for oral rehearsal and student engagement. Each can promote vocabulary, language skills, and increase the volume of writing.

Think About Writing
1. Tell students that authors think about ways they can organize their writing so that their stories make sense and are easy to follow. By adding details, writing becomes much more interesting for readers. Writers explore new ideas and use what they learn for story writing.
2. Review a mentor text if desired, and emphasize the author's use of organization and details.

Teach
3. Tell students, "Today I will show you a tool you can use to organize your thinking when you plan your writing. Writers, your hand is always with you, no matter where you travel. A hand is an awesome organizer. We will call this organizational tool a *Hand Plan*."
4. Show students the palm of your left hand. Use the index finger from your right hand to touch the palm of the outstretched hand and say, "Topic." Flip your hand over so the back of your hand is facing students. Point to each finger (little finger, ring finger, middle finger, and index finger) and say, "Detail," as you touch each one. Finally touch your thumb and say, "Wrap-up." Make certain that you are moving from the students' left to right across your fingers.

Hand Plan (cont.)

5. Tell students the *My Hand Plan* (page 141) can help them organize their ideas for writing. Display a blank *My Hand Plan* or trace your left hand on a sheet of chart paper. Use one of the examples from *Hand Plan Sample* (page 140) to model how to create a *Hand Plan* with ideas for writing. As you model, think aloud so students can hear your thought process while using the Hand Planner. Write only enough so that you can remember your ideas in order to write a sentence on the next writing day. Ideas should be written with words and phrases, not in complete sentences.

Engage

6. Have students *Heads-up, Stand-up, Partner-up* to orally practice their *Hand Plan* for what they will write today. Have them touch their fingers to tell the main idea, details, and wrap-up. Suggest topics from the list of *Topic Ideas* (page 142) if students are having a difficult time coming up with their own.

7. Observe as students work. Remember to move around, look around, and listen. Share ideas you heard during partner discussions that provide support for others. Recognize partners for contributions.

Apply

8. Distribute *My Hand Plan* to students. Have them write in the topic, details, and wrap up their story. Remind students to use *My Hand Plan* as they write today. It will help them to have organized and interesting details they can use when they write.

Write/Conference

9. Provide time for students to write. After students are all settled, rotate around the room conferring with students. Ask questions, such as *What are you working on as a writer? What will you do as a writer when finished with your organizer?*

Spotlight Strategy

10. Choose one or two students who were very successful with the strategy and have them share their ideas with the class.

Share

11. Have students meet with partners to share how they used their *Hand Plan*.

Homework

Ask students to look for interesting topics and create a *Hand Plan* for a story. Encourage students to share their plan with someone at home.

Hand Plan Sample

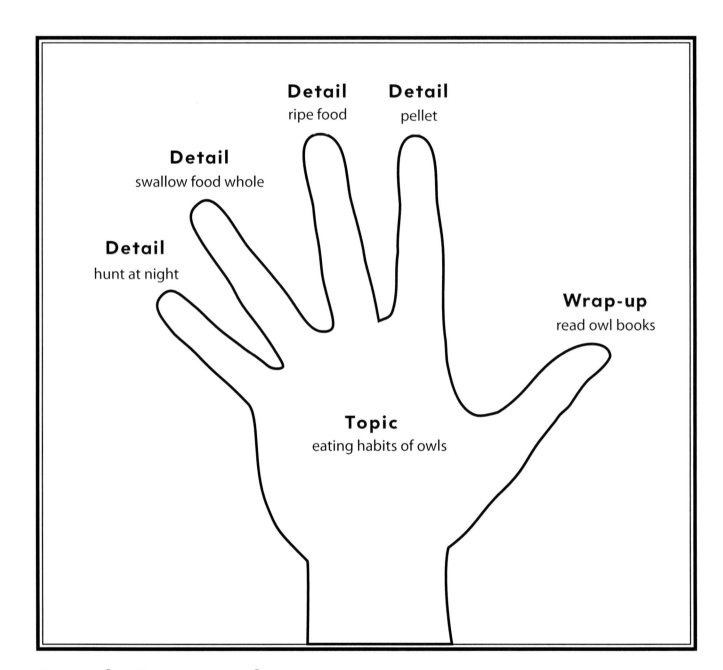

Detail
ripe food

Detail
pellet

Detail
swallow food whole

Detail
hunt at night

Wrap-up
read owl books

Topic
eating habits of owls

Sample Paragraph:

Owls are strange eaters. They are nocturnal, this means they hunt for food at night. When owls find food, they swallow it whole, without chewing. Owls really like ripe, rotten food. When an owl is done eating, it spits out a pellet. A pellet is a hard round ball. If you want to know more about owls, you can read animal books or use the Internet.

Name: _____ Date: _____

My Hand Plan

Directions: Use the hand below to help you plan your writing.

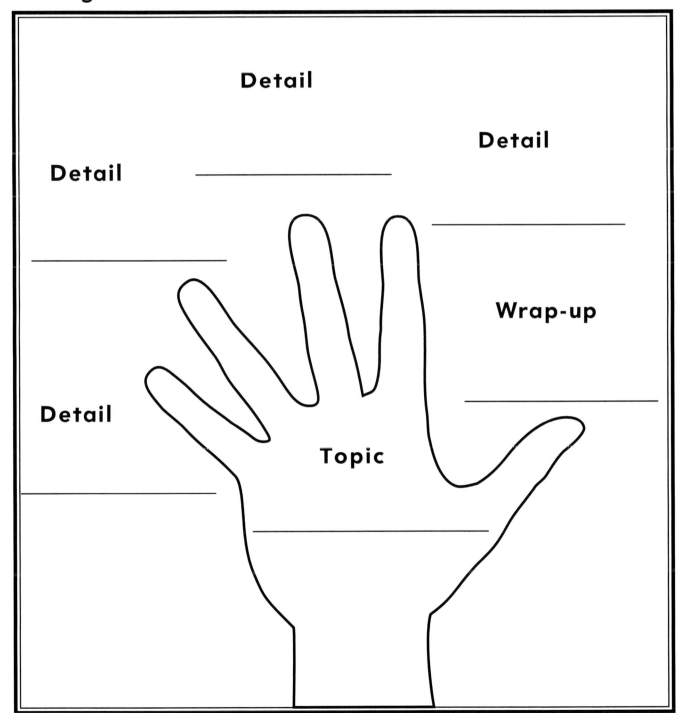

Topic Ideas

Narrative

- Best friends
- Best/Worst experience
- Family fun
- Getting along with others
- Helping others
- Making wishes
- Happy times
- Scary times
- Special people
- Special time/trips
- Working together/ Cooperation

Informative

- Animals and their habitats
- Community helpers
- Other cultures/comparison
- Environment
- Famous/Historical people
- Healthy habits
- Holiday celebrations
- Life Cycles: Frogs, chicks, etc.
- Making healthy snacks
- Our nation's symbols
- Plants and trees
- Safety
- Using manners
- Weather: Wind and storms

Opinion

- Healthy snacks
- Best sports
- My best friend
- My favorite animal
- My favorite family activity
- My favorite holiday
- My favorite story
- My favorite season
- Should we have pets?
- Taking care of others
- The best animal for a pet
- Where you want to live (i.e. city/rural/another country and why)

Telling, Sketching, and Writing Informative Text

Standards
- Uses strategies to organize written work
- Writes in a variety of forms or genres

Materials
- *My Expert List* (page 76; myexpertlist.pdf)
- Chart paper
- Markers
- Sheets of paper stapled together like books *(optional)*
- *Topic Ideas* (page 142; topicideas.pdf)

Mentor Texts
- *The Sun Is My Favorite Star* by Frank Asch
- *Chicks and Chickens* by Gail Gibbons
- *All About Frogs* by Jim Arnosky
- See *Mentor Text List* in Appendix C for other suggestions.

Procedures
Note: This lesson is ideal to use after students have learned about a particular topic. Read aloud nonfiction books to students to help make them experts on topics they can use in their writing. Gail Gibbons and Jim Arnosky are recognized authors of nonfiction for young children. Other grade-level nonfiction text titles may be found at **http://www.corestandards.org**.

Think About Writing
1. Explain to students that there are many ways to gather information and use that information for their writing. As they collect information, the amount of writing they are able to do will increase.

Teach
2. Tell students, "Today I will show you how to write informative text." Explain that to inform means to tell, so informative text tells something.

3. Orally model how to construct an informative paragraph. First, name a topic about which you are an expert, for example, your neighborhood. Use an idea from *My Expert List* (page 76).

4. Think aloud as you give some examples to expand on the topic. For example, "I will tell about the people who have jobs in my neighborhood—mail carrier, teacher, truck driver, grocery clerk, and firefighter." Then, choose one of the examples and think of two details that support it. For example, "A truck driver has to work hard. He makes long trips across the country." The number of details and expectations should increase with your student's writing abilities.

5. Continue modeling how you will wrap up your thinking. For example, "I am glad we have truck drivers to deliver everything."

Telling, Sketching, and Writing
Informative Text *(cont.)*

6. Tell students that now that you have told what you will write, it is time to begin sketching. Remember, a sketch is a quick drawing. Model how to sketch your thoughts and ideas on chart paper. The details from your sketch become the details in your writing. Once your sketch is complete, model using it to develop your writing. Now you have taught them to tell, sketch, and write.

Engage

7. Ask students to think about what they will write. Have them think about all the important information they learned about their topic. Ask students to *Turn and Talk* with partners about the ideas they will use in their writing. Suggest topics from the *Informative* section of *Topic Ideas* (page 142) if students are having a difficult time coming up with their own. Have students share for two minutes. Observe students and choose several to share with the whole group.

Apply

8. Remind students that they can use telling, sketching, and writing to tell about important facts they want a reader to know. Provide students with paper stapled together into books, if desired.

Write/Conference

9. Provide time for students to write. Make important decisions as you become more perceptive at making student observations. Decide who needs additional reteaching and who needs enrichment. Remember to make notes in your Conferring Notebook.

Spotlight Strategy

10. Spotlight a student who is off to a great start. For example, "Extraordinary planning today. Let's stop for just a moment and notice how Xavier is sketching and writing a superb informative text. What a great example for all of us. Writers, you rock!"

Share

11. Select one or two students to share their telling, sketching, and writing work from the Author's Chair. Allow others to share as appropriate.

Homework

Ask students to think about topics on which they are experts. Encourage them to have their families help them. Have them look around their houses for something that might catch their eyes. Tell students to write a list of at least three things on which they are experts.

Telling, Sketching, and Writing Narrative Text

Procedures

Note: This lesson on developing a beginning (B), middle (M), and end (E) can be adapted to topics from your read-aloud literature, Core Reading Program, or titles from the Common Core State Standards reading list. Students' narrative writing may begin with a few sequenced sentences, but needs to advance by the end of the year to include substantial stories.

Think About Writing

1. Remind students they have been building a core of high frequency words so that they can write the words automatically. The room should be filled with think charts to help students gather ideas. They know how to build pattern sentences, using easy patterns, the naming part (subject), and the action part (predicate) to write clear, eloquent sentences. Tell students they have shown an extraordinary ability to write, capturing ideas from other authors to emulate in their own writing.

2. Review mentor texts if desired, and emphasize the author's organization of the story.

Teach

3. Tell students, "Today I will show you how to use your experiences to write a personal narrative." Explain that a personal narrative is a short story about a special time in their lives. Explain that they can gather ideas for personal narratives by making lists of experiences. Narratives can be about a time when they felt happy, scared, sad, or had a really bad day. (*Alexander and the Terrible, Horrible, No Good, Very Bad Day* is great for this lesson.) Narratives can be about lessons they have learned about life.

4. Explain to students that when writing a narrative, answering the questions *Who?*, *What?*, *When?*, *Where?*, and *Why?* will help plan the story. The answers to these questions help create the beginning (B), middle (M), and end (E) of their story.

Telling, Sketching, and Writing Narrative Text *(cont.)*

5. Orally model how to plan your writing by answering the five questions. Come up with your own topic or see *Sample Narratives* (page 147) for ideas for modeling. For example:

Who?	Characters and setting (beginning–B)
What?, When?, and Where?	The body of story including action (middle–M)
Why	Brings closure to the story and wraps-up (ending–E)

Having students answer the five questions and orally practice their stories will add volume to your students' writing and help create personal narratives with beginnings, middles, and endings.

6. On chart paper, model sketching the beginning, middle, and end of the narrative piece you just planned orally. The details from the sketch become the details in the sentences. Once complete, model using your sketch to complete your writing. Now you have told, sketched, and written.

Engage

7. Ask students to think of a topic for writing. Suggest topics from the *Narrative* section of *Topic Ideas* (page 142) if students are having a difficult time coming up with their own. Remind them to use the question words to help create a plan. Have students *Turn and Talk* with partners about their plan for three or four minutes. Have several students share their ideas. This may provide the spark for reluctant writers.

Apply

8. Tell students they can use sketching and writing to tell about their experiences. Remind them to begin by narrowing down their ideas and using some of the small memories of special experiences.

Write/Conference

9. Provide time for students to write. Keep yourself free to walk through the classroom during this lesson. Personal narratives create a whole list of possibilities for conferring, and you want to be free to make notes, provide support, and reteach.

Spotlight Strategy

10. Spotlight a student who has a great beginning to his or her narrative. For example, "London is traveling back in her memory to relive a wonderful experience. You must be exceptionally proud of your ideas and work ethic. Writers, keep rocking!"

Share

11. Invite one or two students to share their telling, sketching, and writing in the Author's Chair.

Homework

Ask students to sketch three pictures that show what will happen in their narrative—one for the beginning, one for the middle, and one for the end.

Sample Narratives

Simple Text

(Use temporary spelling for difficult words, but write high frequency words fast and smooth as you model.)

My daughter, Jasmine, had a pair of hamsters in a cage. One summer day, both hamsters escaped and decided to live in the kitchen, behind the refrigerator. They chewed through the ice maker tubes and water line. It took us forever to catch them, and the damage from their escape was very expensive. That was a terrible week for our family.

Simple Text with Time Cue Words

My daughter, Jasmine, had a pair of hamsters. One day they jumped out of their cage. Next, they hid behind the refrigerator. Then, we caught them and put them back into their cage. It ended up being known as The Great Hamster Rescue!

Using Speech Bubbles

Standards

- Uses strategies to organize written work
- Writes in a variety of forms or genres

Materials

- Comic strips with speech bubbles
- Drawing paper

Mentor Texts

- *Knuffle Bunny* or *Knuffle Bunny Too* by Mo Willems
- See *Mentor Text List* in Appendix C for other suggestions.

Procedures

Note: Speech bubbles are used to express ideas, such as "I like pizza the best" (opinion); "I can ride my bike" (narrative); and "Mars is a planet" (informative).

Think About Writing

1. Tell students that writers work on developing organizational strategies and patterns of writing to express their ideas, thoughts, and feelings. Authors use cartoons, books, and other means to communicate. Writing in different ways using different text types makes writing interesting, full of energy, and fun. Many authors use speech bubbles as a way to capture their audience.

Teach

2. Tell students, "Today I will show you a fun, interesting way to write using speech bubbles to communicate what story characters are thinking or saying."

3. Show students several examples of mentor texts and emphasize the authors' use of speech bubbles in books. Also, bring comic strips from the newspaper as additional examples.

4. Show students how to fold a sheet of paper in half and then in half again. Open the paper so that four sections are showing. Model how to draw pictures in each section and use speech bubbles to show what story characters are thinking or saying.

Engage

5. Ask students to think of an idea they will write about. Then, have them *Turn and Talk* to partners about their story ideas. Provide approximately two minutes for students to gather and share their ideas.

Using Speech Bubbles (cont.)

Apply

6. Tell students that authors often experiment with different forms of writing like using speech bubbles to express a character's thinking. It is fun to use a variety of writing techniques. Distribute paper to students and ensure they fold it correctly.

Write/Conference

7. Provide time for students to write. Rotate around the room and look for any confusion. Reteach in a small group format with modeling when needed. Then continue to confer with students. Remember to praise, compliment, and teach as you meet with students. Remember to keep anecdotal observations to inform your instructional decision making on the next writing day.

Spotlight Strategy

8. Spotlight a student who has used speech bubbles effectively. For example, "Please notice how Atif sketched ideas first, then added speech bubbles to inform the reader of the message. Superb thinking!"

Share

9. Provide approximately two minutes for students to meet with partners to share their work.

Homework

Ask students to find and bring to school at least one example of speech bubbles being used in text.

Writing a Letter

Standards

- Uses strategies to organize written work
- Writes in a variety of forms or genres

Materials

- Chart paper
- Markers
- Letters
- *My Friendly Letter* (page 152; myfriendlyletter.pdf)

Mentor Texts

- *I Wanna Iguana* by Karen Kaufman Orloff
- *I Wanna New Room* by Karen Kaufman Orloff
- *Yours Truly, Goldilocks* by Alma Ada
- See *Mentor Text List* in Appendix C for other suggestions.

Procedures

Note: You may wish to read a variety of texts prior to introducing letter writing to build understanding. Revisit the mini-lesson to write to grandparents, sports figures, school personnel, friends, and literary characters.

Think About Writing

1. Tell students that books are a great place to get ideas for writing. By looking at how authors have organized their books, we can get ideas for different ways we can organize our writing.

2. Review mentor texts if desired, emphasizing the author's organization of the book into letters or notes. For example, in *I Wanna Iguana*, Karen Orloff writes about a conversation between a mom and her son, except the conversation is all written in the form of letters. Alex's friend is moving and cannot take his pet Iguana. So, guess what Alex is writing to his mother about in this story?

Teach

3. Tell students, "Today I will show you how to write a simple letter to your family or friends." Share samples of letters, cards, thank you notes, and postcards.

4. Tell students that letters are written in a very special way and include some parts that are different from the stories they have been writing. A letter written correctly has five basic parts:

   Heading: The heading is located in the upper right-hand corner and includes the date.

   Greeting: The greeting usually begins with *Dear*, then the person's name. Always use a comma after the greeting.

   Body: The body is the message of your letter—what you want to say to your reader.

Writing a Letter *(cont.)*

Closing: The closing tells the reader you are finishing your thoughts.

Signature: Sign your name directly below the closing.

5. Model writing a letter on a sheet of chart paper. Use correct, friendly letter format and provide options for the greeting and closing. Label each section of the letter. Post the anchor chart for display.

6. Have students practice each part of the letter using the *My Turn, Your Turn* format (page 276).

Engage

7. Have students *Turn and Talk* to partners and use their five fingers to review the letter parts with their partners.

8. Ask students to think about a letter they would like to write. Have them talk with partners about what they will include in their letters. Ask each of the following questions, allowing time for students to discuss the answers with partners, and then move on to the next question: "To whom would you send a letter?"; "What date will you put on your letter?"; "What greeting will you use?"; " What might you say in your message?"; "How will you close and sign your letter?"

Apply

9. Tell students that one way to communicate is to use notes and letters. Remind students they may want to write thank you notes for gifts received, invitations to parties, or even a letter to the newspaper. Ask students to think about their partner discussions while they are writing their note or letter.

Write/Conference

10. Distribute *My Friendly Letter* (page 152). Provide time for students to write. This will be a new format for many students. Be ready to problem solve for anyone who may have confusion. Use your Conferring Notebook for observations.

Spotlight Strategy

11. Spotlight a student with a good example of a letter. For example, "James got right to work and has accomplished so much writing in such a short amount of time. James, please share your letter with our group! Remarkable writing work!"

Share

12. Have students meet with partners to share their notes or letters. Select one or two students to share in the Author's Chair. This is a new genre and having students correctly model the format is a powerful teacher to the other students.

Homework

Ask students to bring to school the address of someone they would like to send a letter to.

Name: _____ Date: _____

My Friendly Letter

Directions: Write a friendly letter in the space below.

_____

Dear _____,

_____

_____

_____

_____

_____

_____

_____

Sincerely,

_____

Addressing an Envelope

Standard

Writes in a variety of forms or genres

Materials

- Chart paper
- Markers
- Envelopes

Mentor Texts

- *The Jolly Postman* by Allan and Janet Ahlberg
- *Click, Clack, Moo* by Doreen Cronin
- See *Mentor Text List* in Appendix C for other suggestions.

Procedures

Think About Writing

1. Write a letter on chart paper to students using the letter format from the previous lesson and read the letter aloud to students. For example:

   Dear Students,

   We have spent a few days writing letters to friends, family, school personnel, famous people, and sports figures. Letter writing is something everyone needs to know how to do. Grown-ups are required to write letters, notes, and cards during their lives. I write business letters, notes to children and their parents, notes and cards to friends and relatives, and even letters to the editor of newspapers. You, too, will write lots of letters.

   Sincerely,

   Your name

2. Review mentor texts if desired, and emphasize the addresses on the envelopes.

Teach

3. Tell students, "Today I will show you how to address an envelope so you can mail your letters." Explain that *address* means that we write the name and residence or location of the person to whom the letter is being sent. Usually, the location includes a house number, a street name, the city, the state, and the zip code.

Addressing an Envelope *(cont.)*

4. Model for students how to address an envelope. Write your name and address in the upper-left-hand corner of the envelope. In the upper-right-hand corner of the envelope, place a stamp or draw one if the envelope will not be mailed. Halfway down in the middle of the envelope and slightly to the left side, write the complete name and address of the person to whom you are writing. Separate the name of the city from the state with a comma and make the state a two-letter abbreviation; both letters should be capitals and no period at the end.

Engage

5. Ask students to *Turn and Talk* with partners about the procedure for addressing an envelope. Encourage them to clear up any confusion before they begin to work.

Apply

6. Remind students that sending letters is an excellent way to use their writing skills and share their thoughts with others. Letter writing and envelope addressing are life skills that they will use regularly as they move through school and through life.

Write/Conference

7. Provide time for students to work on their envelopes. Remind them, as you conference, about the correct placement of return address, address, etc.

Spotlight Strategy

8. Spotlight a student who had a nicely addressed envelope. For example, "Please turn and look at the beautiful envelope addressed by Annika. When I finish showing Annika's envelope, please give her a round of applause."

Share

9. Have students meet with partners to share the envelopes they addressed today. Remind students to provide lots of compliments to their partners.

Homework

Ask students to talk with their families about letter writing. Have them ask if their parents address envelopes to pay bills, to write to family members, or to stay in touch with a friend. Have students list all the ways their families use addressed envelopes.

I Know How To...

Standard

Writes in a variety of forms or genres

Materials

- Chart paper
- Markers
- *How to Planner* (page 157; howtoplanner.pdf)
- 3" × 5" index cards
- Peanut butter (or jelly if a "nut-free" environment)
- Bread
- Napkin
- Butter knife

Mentor Texts

- *Peanut Butter and Jelly: A Play Rhyme* by Nadine B. Westcott
- *Pancakes for Breakfast* by Tomie dePaola
- *Training a Guide Dog* by Wendy MacDonald
- samples of game instructions
- recipe books
- See *Mentor Text List* in Appendix C for other suggestions.

Procedures

Note: Be sure to share many examples of how-to books prior to modeling this genre. Allow adequate time to model, explore topic choices, plan, draft, and write. This is a fun writing piece to publish for a class book titled *We Know How To…*

Think About Writing

1. Review a mentor text if desired. Remind students they have been experimenting with many *genres*, or kinds of writing. They have written letters, studied other authors to get ideas, created thinking charts, and learned to use speech bubbles. Explain that a *how-to* is an important genre of writing and is useful in real life. This genre of writing helps us learn to do new things. Authors of *how-to* writing know a lot about their subjects. They are experts in that area. Remind students they are all experts at something they can share with readers!

Teach

2. Tell students, "Today I will show you how to write directions for making a peanut butter and jelly sandwich." Explain that when providing directions, it is helpful to include words to show the sequence of events. Write the words *first*, *then*, *next*, and *last* on index cards. Discuss each word and then display the words in the classroom.

3. Model creating a real peanut butter and jelly sandwich. After modeling each step, move to chart paper (or use the *How-to Planner* on page 157) and create simple illustrations, words, and phrases for that step. Repeat for each step. Use the think-aloud below and on the next page to model how to create the sandwich.

   First, I need to get my supplies. (peanut butter, jelly, bread, napkin, dull knife)

   Then, I place a slice of bread on my napkin and spread peanut butter to all of the corners of the bread.

I Know How To... (cont.)

Next, I take a second slice of bread and smother it with jelly.

Last, I put the two pieces together and enjoy my delicious snack!

4. Build a class idea chart of *Things We Know How to Do*. Review sequence words and their use. Give partners time to discuss and choose their individual topics before moving on to the planning.

Engage

5. Ask students to *Turn and Talk* to partners to orally plan their writing. Have students talk over four fingers using the order words to help organize their thoughts: *first*, *then*, *next*, and *last*.

Apply

6. Remind students to explore the newly introduced genre of *how-to* in their writing. Have students choose a how-to idea from the anchor chart of ideas. Distribute the *How-to Planner* to students and tell them they can use this page to describe their steps to readers.

Write/Conference

7. Provide time for students to write. Remember to take the time to really listen to your students. Confirm what they have already done accurately, and make suggestions for new thinking. Remember to write down your thoughts in your Conferring Notebook.

Spotlight Strategy

8. Call attention to one or two students who have grasped writing a *how-to* piece and spotlight their work.

Share

9. Have students meet in triads. Ask them to take turns sharing their *how-to* writing. Encourage students to listen carefully to their partners and see if the directions are clear (easy to follow). Remind students to compliment and question each other.

Homework

Ask students to make a list of three other ideas for *how-to* books. Remind students they are all experts at something.

Name: _____ Date: _____

How-to Planner

Directions: Use the chart below to plan your *how-to* story. Then write the story on the lines provided.

First	Next
Then	**Last**

_____

_____

_____

_____

_____

_____

Poetry: Simple Acrostic

Standards

- Uses strategies to organize written work
- Writes in a variety of forms or genres

Materials

- Chart paper
- Markers

Mentor Texts

- *Autumn: An Alphabet Acrostic* by Steven Schnur (Also, *Winter, Spring,* and *Summer*)
- See *Mentor Text List* in Appendix C for other suggestions.

Procedures

Note: You may wish to develop an acrostic poem with the whole class using the same topic. Students also enjoy working with partners to develop their poetry. Challenge students to add a line or two of alliteration (words with the same beginning sound).

Think About Writing

1. Remind students they have been writing about their personal experiences and telling what happened by creating images in the reader's mind. These types of stories are written to entertain. Sometimes authors entertain the reader by using wordplay to create an acrostic poem.

2. Review a mentor text if desired, and emphasize the author's organization of the text in acrostic poems.

Teach

3. Tell students, "Today I will show you how to create an acrostic poem to entertain your readers." Explain that acrostics are a fun, simple, and easy to write. In an acrostic poem, a word is written vertically down the page and each letter is the beginning sound for a new word or short phrase. Names, places, animals, or anything you can imagine can be used for the acrostic word.

4. Explain that the first thing to do is choose a word or topic and write it vertically down the side of the paper. Model on chart paper an acrostic poem using the word *KITE*.

5. Ask students to help generate words and/or a short phrase that begin with each letter of the word. For example:

K	I	T	E
kids toy	it's dipping and diving	touching the clouds	ending
kind of fun	interesting	toy	entertaining
keeps going	into the trees	teetering	extra colorful
kids	in the sky	tail waving	exciting

Poetry: Simple Acrostic (cont.)

6. Choose one of the words or phrases for each line and write out the acrostic poem on the chart paper. See the examples below.

Word Acrostic	Mixed Word/Phrase
Kids	**K**atie's
Interesting	**I**n the sky
Toy	**T**ail waving
Exciting	**E**xciting!

Challenge with Alliteration
Katie's kite
Incredible indigo
Tiny tail
Exciting, enjoyable!

Engage

7. Ask students to think of a topic word for their own acrostic poem. Have students *Heads-up, Stand-up, Partner-up* and work with partners to share their topics and brainstorm some ideas for each letter in the word. Remind students to take turns and give each other ideas.

Apply

8. Remind students that acrostic poems are one way to entertain readers by using wordplay. Ask students to remember to use the example and what they shared with their partners as they write their own acrostic poems.

Write/Conference

9. Provide time for students to write. Rotate around the room to observe and assist students needing support. Gather a small group to create a group poem, if needed. Use your Conferring Notebook to note student growth and needs.

Spotlight Strategy

10. Spotlight a student who has a great example of an acrostic poem. For example, "I am so excited to share with you. Catelyn is using very descriptive words to describe her topic, just like a real poet."

Share

11. Have students meet with partners to share their poetry. Remind students to listen for describing words and to give compliments.

Homework

Ask students to make a list of five words they might use to make an acrostic poem.

Poetry: Five Ws Poem

Standards

- Uses strategies to organize written work
- Writes in a variety of forms or genres

Materials

- Index cards
- Markers
- *5 Ws Poem Planner* (page 162; 5wspoemplanner.pdf)
- Chart paper

Mentor Texts

- *Here's a Little Poem: A Very First Book of Poetry* by Jane Yolen
- *Read Aloud Rhymes for the Very Young* by Jack Prelutsky
- *Where the Sidewalk Ends* by Shel Silverstein
- See *Mentor Text List* in Appendix C for other suggestions.

Procedures

Note: Like other genres, students need to be exposed to lots of poetry prior to instruction. Read a poem a day and briefly discuss what you notice in the poems, such as the topic, words, flow of the language, and feelings/voice.

Think About Writing

1. Remind students there are many different genres or kinds of writing, like informative, narrative, letter writing, and even poetry. Poetry is one way authors share their thoughts and feelings. There are many different kinds of poems and today we will explore a poem pattern.

2. Review a mentor text if desired, and emphasize the organization of the text as a poem.

Teach

3. Tell students, "Today I will show you how to create a *5 Ws Poem*." Explain that a *5 Ws Poem* is a patterned poem that tells *who*, *what*, *when*, *where*, and *why*. Write each word on an index card and display the words for students to see.

4. Tell students that the first step is to choose one idea that they can write about. Examples include: sports, friends, family, etc. Then, find one specific thing about the idea (to go in the why section). Next, read the 5 Ws question words and write a quick response to each question. Tell students to write each response on a different line.

5. Model each step of creating a 5 Ws poem on a sheet of chart paper or on the *5 Ws Poem Planner* (page 162). For example:

Who?	My dog	The sun
What?	Loves to play ball	Shines brightly
When?	On Saturdays	Early in the morning
Where?	In my backyard	Across my sleepy face
Why?	He loves to run and jump!	Telling me, "Wake up!"

Poetry: Five Ws Poem *(cont.)*

Engage

6. Have students *Heads-up, Stand-up, Partner-up*. Tell students they will create their own 5 Ws poem. Ask students to think of a topic they will write about and consider the 5 Ws questions. Then, using their five fingers, explain their thinking to their partners.

Apply

7. Remind students there are many ways to express themselves using poetry as well as other genres of writing. Show them the 5 Ws planner and show them where to write and also where to illustrate their poem.

Write/Conference

8. Distribute the *5Ws Poem Planner*. Provide time for students to write. Scan the classroom to determine if everyone knows how to begin. Confer with individuals or small groups and use your observations to establish a starting point.

Spotlight Strategy

9. Choose one or two students from the group that appear to have applied the mini-lesson in their writing and spotlight their work.

Share

10. Have students meet with partners to share their poems. Review with students how share time needs to look and sound so it remains a productive time. Remind students to give each other feedback, including compliments and questions.

Homework

Ask students to show their families how to use their five fingers and the five question words to generate new ideas they can use during their writing time tomorrow. Encourage students to challenge someone in their families to create a 5 Ws poem with them.

Name: _____ Date: _____

5 Ws Poem Planner

Directions: Write your answers to the questions. Then, make an illustration to go with your 5 Ws poem. Cover up the questions and you'll have your poem.

Who?	
What?	
When?	
Where?	
Why?	

Word Choice
Showing Not Telling

A writer's use of rich, descriptive words can visually show the reader a mental image. By studying word choice, students will learn how to use vivid, colorful, and dynamic words to enrich their writing and make it as precise as possible. The use of amazing words is encouraged; however, everyday words used correctly are also celebrated. These lessons assist students in exploring different types of words and the ways they can be used to create interest in writing pieces. Lessons in this section include the following:

- Lesson 1: Using High Frequency Words (page 165)
- Lesson 2: Using Words to Paint a Picture (page 169)
- Lesson 3: More Than Big and Little (page 173)
- Lesson 4: I Say It with My Senses (page 176)
- Lesson 5: Awesome Adjectives (page 182)
- Lesson 6: Show Me: Using Action Words (page 184)
- Lesson 7: Amazing Words (page 187)
- Lesson 8: Transition Words (page 190)
- Lesson 9: Sounds All Around from A to Z (page 195)

The *Wally, Word Choice Detective* poster (page 164) can be displayed in the room to provide a visual reminder for students that word choice is one of the traits of writing. You may wish to introduce this poster during the first lesson on word choice. Then, refer to the poster when teaching other lessons on word choice to refresh students' memories and provide them with questions to guide them as they make choices for words they use in their writing.

Wally
Word Choice
Detective

What words will paint a picture for my reader?

✔ Did I use some *amazing* words?

✔ Did I use sensory words?

✔ Did I use action words?

✔ Did I use a variety of words?

Using High Frequency Words

Standard

Uses conventions of spelling in written compositions

Materials

- Chart paper
- Marker
- *Learn a Word Chart* (page 167; learnwordchart.pdf)
- *High Frequency Word List* (page 168; highfreqwordlist.pdf)

Mentor Text

- Poems
- Nursery rhymes
- See *Mentor Text List* in Appendix C for other suggestions.

Procedures

Note: There are many variations on high-frequency word lists. Use the one included with this lesson or one your school or district uses.

Think About Writing

1. Tell students that writers learn to use tools to improve their writing. It is useful to have a list of words we can write automatically (without thinking). Writers use strategies and tools to spell words, find words, and build words.

2. Review a mentor text if desired, and emphasize the author's use of word choice.

Teach

3. Tell students, "Today I will teach you a strategy to build a core of words that you can write quickly and smoothly." Display *Learn a Word Chart* (page 167) to provide visual support to the steps you will teach students so they can learn the word.

4. Choose a word from the *High Frequency Word List* (page 168). Write the word on a sheet of chart paper. Model the first three bullets and invite students to join in on the "Write it" and "Check it" sections.

   - Say, "See it!" Point to the left of the word. Students should look at the word and think it in their heads. Provide a few seconds for students to look at the word.
   - Say, "Say it!" Slide your finger under the word as you say the word.
   - Say, "Spell it!" Tap your finger under each letter. As you tap each letter, say the letter name as you spell the word.

Using High Frequency Words *(cont.)*

- Say, "Write it!" Have students pretend one hand is paper and the index finger of the other hand is a pencil. Students write the word on their hands three times quickly and smoothly. Move around and observe, providing corrective feedback to any student making incorrect letter strokes.
- Say, "Check it!" Find the word on the chart paper and check the spelling.

Practice additional words until students are familiar with the procedure.

Engage

5. Have students practice *See it! Say it! Spell it! Write it! Check it!* with partners. Remind students it helps them become better spellers for writing. Provide students additional words to practice. Monitor partners and provide support when needed.

Apply

6. Remind students good writers write with automaticity, quickly and smoothly. Tell students, "This activity will help make your writing easier and make you a better speller for writing projects." Tell students when they have finished their word practice, they can choose an idea and begin writing.

Write/Conference

7. Provide time for students to write. Scan the room to be certain students understand. Then rotate among students and support their efforts with questions and comments.

Spotlight Strategy

8. Spotlight great student work. For example, "What a genius! Alexis is using the word chart and is practicing See it! Say it! Spell it! Write it! Check it! Good writers use all the tools around them to help them write words."

Share

9. Have students meet with partners. Ask them to show their partners some words they can write quickly and smoothly. Have students practice those words together.

Homework

Ask students to think about how letters, sounds, words, and language are all around them. Encourage them to grow their word knowledge by making a list of ten words, finding words in newspapers and magazines, and be ready to share their thinking tomorrow in Writer's Workshop.

Learn a Word Chart

See it!	like
Say it!	like
Spell it!	l-i-k-e
Write it!	like
Check it!	like

High Frequency Word List

Words I Use in My Writing						
A a	**B b**	**C c**	**D d**	**E e**	**F f**	**G g**	**H h**
a about after all and are as ask at	be because big boy but by	came can cat come could	dad day did do dog don't down	eat	find fly for friend from fun funny	get give go going good	had has have he her here him his home house
I i	**J j**	**K k**	**L l**	**M m**	**N n**	**O o**	**P p**
I if in is it	jump just	kids	like little live look love	make may me mom more must my	no not	of on open or other our out over	people play please pretty
Q q-R r	**S s**	**T t**		**U u-V v**	**W w**		**Xx-Yy-Zz**
ran ride round run	said saw say school see she so some soon stop	thank that the them then there they things this	time to too	under up us very	walk was we went were what when where	will with would	yes you

—adapted from Teaching Kids to Spell, Gentry (1993) and Teaching Primary Reading, Dolch (1941)

Using Words to Paint a Picture

Standards

- Uses descriptive words to convey basic ideas
- Uses writing and other methods to describe familiar persons, places, objects, or experiences

Materials

- Chart paper
- Marker
- *Color Words* (page 171; colorwords.pdf)
- *Number Words* (page 172; numberwords.pdf)

Mentor Texts

- *A Color of His Own* by Leo Lionni
- *Color Dance* by Ann Jonas
- *Pete the Cat: I Love My White Shoes* by Eric Litwin
- See *Mentor Text List* in Appendix C for other suggestions.

Procedures

Note: This mini-lesson may be adapted to explore additional descriptive and describing word charts, such as size words, seasonal words, birthday words, emotion words, etc. Create anchor charts for different categories of words for students to refer to as they write.

Think About Writing

1. Tell students that writers add energy and excitement to their writing projects by using words and sentences to create delightful stories. Authors use just the right words, so readers can see the story in their minds. Beginning writers learn to use simple color, number, and size words before moving on to other challenging words.

2. Review a mentor text if desired, and emphasize color, number, and size words. For example, read portions of *A Color of His Own* and have students give thumbs up when they hear words that paint pictures in their minds, such as color or number words.

Teach

3. Tell students, "Today I will show you how to use things at your fingertips to make a word painting of your ideas." Have students assist you in developing an anchor chart of color words from the mentor texts you have read.

4. Write the following story on chart paper:

   My redheaded daughter was doing flips on the prickly green grass in the yard. A black skunk with white brushed streaks waddled to where she was playing. Calee rushed into the house and grabbed a small, red carton of cereal. The striped baby skunk nestled softly in her hand and ate every brown, crumbly bite. Now the skunk has become a pest and hides in the yellow dandelions.

Using Words to Paint a Picture *(cont.)*

5. Distribute *Color Words* (page 171) to students. Have students identify the color in the circles with the appropriate color as they hear them in the story.

Engage

6. Have students close their eyes as you reread the story. Ask them to make a movie about what is happening in their minds.

7. Ask students to *Turn and Talk* with partners about how the color words created a mind picture for them as they listened.

8. Have students talk with partners about how they plan to use words that will paint a picture in their readers' minds. Provide approximately two minutes for partners to talk.

Apply

9. Then, have students complete the charts on *Color Words* and *Number Words* (pages 171–172) by writing additional color words they know. Allow students time to complete these before they begin writing. Tell students that they may write on a topic of their choice. Remind students to use words that will help their reader make mind pictures. Students may keep *Color Words* and *Number Words* in their folders for future reference.

Write/Conference

10. Provide time for students to write. Scan your group for student engagement and work ethic. Then, observe and confer with students about their work.

Spotlight Strategy

11. Spotlight a student who is using colorful words. For example, "Writers, perfect thinking and planning. Listen to Jenny's use of colorful words."

Share

12. Have students meet with partners who are wearing the same color as they are. Tell students that by the time your fingers count to three, they should be meeting with that colorful partner to share their finest examples. Remind students to provide a compliment.

Homework

Ask students to look around their homes at all the amazing colors. Remind students that these colors can be added to their writing folders and can be used in their writing. Ask students to come tomorrow ready to share their discoveries!

Name: _____ Date: _____

Color Words

Directions: Color the circles for each color. Write more color words on the lines provided.

red	blue	yellow	green	orange
○	○	○	○	○
purple	**pink**	**black**	**white**	**brown**
○	○	○	○	○

More Color Words I Know

Name: _____ Date: _____

Number Words

Directions: Write more number words that you know on the lines provided.

1 one	2 two	3 three	4 four	5 five
6 six	7 seven	8 eight	9 nine	10 ten

More Number Words I Know

More Than Big and Little

Standards

- Uses descriptive words to convey basic ideas
- Uses writing and other methods to describe familiar persons, places, objects, or experiences

Materials

- Chart paper
- Markers
- *Size Words* (page 175; sizewords.pdf)

Mentor Texts

- *Big, Bigger, Biggest!* by Nancy Coffelt
- *Big and Little* by Steve Jenkins
- *How Big Is It?* by Ben Hillman
- *Max's Words* by Kate Banks
- See *Mentor Text List* in Appendix C for other suggestions.

Procedures

Note: This lesson may be repeated to develop additional student word banks, for example, good/bad.

Think About Writing

1. Tell students that writers grow by developing their writing ideas and creating super sentences that are interesting for their readers. Explain that it is important for writers to select just the right words to show their readers mental images of the stories. As beginning writers, sometimes the same words are used again and again in our stories.

2. Review a mentor text if desired, and emphasize the author's use of interesting words. For example, Nancy Coffelt uses many interesting words in her writing.

Teach

3. Tell students, "Today I will show you how to create even more interesting stories by using synonyms." Explain that a *synonym* is a word that means almost the same as another word; it is similar. Review a mentor text and emphasize the synonyms the author uses. For example, the hippo in *Big, Bigger, Biggest* is big—*large*, *huge*, *jumbo*. Tell students these are all words that can be used for *big*. Good writers use just the right word to help their readers understand exactly what they are thinking.

4. Sketch an elephant and a mouse on a sheet of chart paper. Write *big* next to the elephant and *little* next to the mouse. Then, think aloud and add a few synonyms for each word, for example: *gigantic*, *jumbo*, *teeny*, and *miniature*.

More Than Big and Little (cont.)

Engage

5. Have students *Heads-up, Stand-up, Partner-up*. Ask students to think about the words they hear all around. Have them share synonyms for big and little with their partners. Challenge pairs to think of five words for *big* and five for *little*.

6. Have students share their words and add them to the class chart.

Apply

7. Remind students to use words that tell their readers exactly what they want the reader to see.

8. Distribute *Size Words* (page 175) to students to put in their writing folders. Tell students they will be writing on a topic of their choice. Remind students to use synonyms to make their writing more exciting.

Write/Conference

9. Provide time for students to write. Check your Conferring Notebook to make certain you are visiting all students. Take notes on possible spotlighting targets as you move around. Help individual students find words in their writing that can be replaced with synonyms. Remember to give individual praise also.

Spotlight Strategy

10. Spotlight a student who has used an author as a model. For example, "Listen to how Melissa has used words just like (an author you used as a mentor text)." Name specifically what the student did to be clear and precise.

Share

11. Have students take one minute to check their writing for interesting words. Then, have students work with partners to share their writing. Challenge students to look for interesting words their partners used.

Homework

Ask students to listen to conversation, talk from adults, TV, or anything or anyone else and be on the lookout for descriptive words that make writing interesting. Have students make lists of at least five words they hear, and ask them to be ready to share their lists in Writer's Workshop.

Name: _____ Date: _____

Size Words

little

- small
- tiny
- wee
- itty bitty
- mini
- teeny
- toy

big

- large
- grand
- huge
- giant
- jumbo
- gigantic
- enormous

A Few More Size Words

- tall
- short
- long
- average

I Say It with My Senses

Standards

- Uses descriptive words to convey basic ideas
- Uses writing and other methods to describe familiar persons, places, objects, or experiences

Materials

- Chart paper
- Markers
- *Five Senses Words* (page 178; fivesenseswords.pdf)
- *Say It with Senses!* (page 179; sayitwithsenses.pdf)
- *Senses Picture Cards* (pages 180–181; sensespicturecards.pdf)
- Chocolate sandwich cookie

Mentor Texts

- *Hello Ocean* by Pam Muñoz Ryan
- *My Five Senses* by Aliki
- *What You Know First* by Patricia MacLachlan
- See *Mentor Text List* in Appendix C for other suggestions.

Procedures

Note: You may wish to bring in some actual items for student engagement and application.

Think About Writing

1. Tell students that good writers read and learn new ways to improve their writing from other authors.

2. Review a mentor text if desired, and emphasize the sensory words the author uses. For example, Pam Muñoz Ryan is a master at using words to describe the ocean in *Hello Ocean*. The main character, a young girl, splendidly describes the ocean using her five senses. The author makes it seem like you are right in the middle of her story. Read this book aloud if possible.

Teach

3. Tell students, "Today I will show you how to examine the things around you and use your five senses to write words that create images for your readers."

4. Use the *Five Senses Words* (page 178) to review each of the five senses with students.

5. Show students the chocolate sandwich cookie. Display *Say It with Senses* (page 179) and tell students this page will help organize their sensory words about the cookie. Think aloud as you explore and record your ideas about the cookie. For example:

   - I *see*—round like a coin, brown on the top and bottom, white in the middle.
   - I *smell*—sweet like chocolate, yummy.
   - It *feels*—rough on the top and bottom, gooey in the middle.
   - It *tastes*—scrumptious and sweet.
   - It *sounds*— crunchy when I chew it.

I Say It with My Senses *(cont.)*

Engage

6. Display *Senses Picture Cards* (pages 180–181) one at a time. Have students *Heads-up, Stand-up, Partner-up* and work with partners to discuss each picture and describe it using their five senses. Allow time for discussion between each picture. You may also wish to have students discuss one picture at a time to help keep them organized.

Apply

7. Distribute *Say It With Senses!* to students. Have them choose a picture or object and complete the chart.

8. Remind students that using their five senses helps them think of words that will show the readers their stories. They will use their five senses to write about a topic of their choice. Make magazine pictures, *Five Senses Word s,* or the *Senses Picture Cards* available for students to use while they are writing.

Write/Conference

9. Provide time for students to write. Pull a small group of students for a guided writing lesson to reteach skills based on observations of writing. Use anecdotal notes of writing behaviors to plan future instruction.

Spotlight Strategy

10. Spotlight a student who uses great descriptive language. For example, "You are using brilliant descriptive language. Notice how Evan tapped into his brain and made great choices adding sensory words to his writing."

Share

11. Have students work with partners to choose two sensory words to share with the group. Provide approximately two minutes for partners to share.

12. Gather students back together and have partners share their words. Write the words on an anchor chart that can be posted in the classroom so it is visible when students are writing. Remind students that new words can be added to the chart throughout the year.

Homework

Ask students to notice the world around them. Provide students with an additional copy of *Say It with Senses* and have them choose one object and use their five senses.

Five Senses Words

My 5 Senses Words

I see...

I hear...

I smell...

I taste...

I feel...

#50915—Core of Writing—Level 1

Name: _____ Date: _____

Say It with Senses!

Directions: Write the object or picture you are examining in the first row. Use your senses to write ideas about it in the spaces provided.

I am examining...	
I see...	
I hear...	
I smell...	
I taste...	
I feel...	

Senses Picture Cards

Teacher Directions: Create copies of the *Senses Picture Cards*. Have students describe each card using their senses.

Senses Picture Cards (cont.)

Awesome Adjectives

Standards

- Uses descriptive words to convey basic ideas
- Uses adjectives in written compositions

Materials

- Chart paper
- Marker
- Sticky notes or word cards

Mentor Texts

- *Chrysanthemum* by Kevin Henkes
- *The Big Yawn* by Kevin Faulkner
- *That's My Dog* by Rick Walton
- See *Mentor Text List* in Appendix C for other suggestions.

Procedures

Note: You may wish to compile noun and adjective anchor charts from mentor texts you have read. For example, in *The Big Yawn*, the noun (*mouth*) and the adjectives (*scaly, gigantic, toothy,* and *tremendous*) could be added to the anchor chart.

Think About Writing

1. Tell students that the words an author uses in writing create mental images for the readers.

2. Review a mentor text if desired, and emphasize the mental images that the author creates using words. For example, in *Chrysanthemum*, Kevin Henkes uses the words: *sunniest dress, brightest smile, pleasant dream,* and *comfortable jumper.*

Teach

3. Tell students, "Today I will show you how to use words that paint a picture for your reader. We will do this by adding descriptive words in front of the names of objects, people, and places (nouns). They can make our writing more interesting." Tell students they will help create a list of awesome adjectives.

4. Write the following list of nouns on a sheet of chart paper: *car, cat, dog, girl, boy, book,* and *desk.* Leave room in front of each word to add an adjective.

5. Have students create a picture in their heads of the word *car.* Ask if their picture of a car changes if we ask the question: What kind of car? Write the adjective *speedy* on a sticky note and place it in front of the word *car.* Discuss how the adjective changes the picture in students' heads. Continue adding adjectives in front of the list of nouns. Discuss with students the effect the adjective has. Adjective and noun examples include: *speeding car, calico cat, barking dog, crying girl, mischievous boy, interesting book, and messy desk.*

#50915—Core of Writing—Level 1

Awesome Adjectives (cont.)

6. Model for students how to create a sentence using the words *speedy car*. Have students create sentences using other adjective and noun pairs.

Engage

7. Write a noun on a sheet of chart paper. Suggested nouns include: *tiger*, *baby*, and *shoes*. Have students *Heads-up, Stand-up, Partner-up* and work together to think of adjectives to describe the noun.

8. Ask students to create sentences using the adjective and noun. As students are talking, move around the group to listen to and take notes on students' sentences. Have several pairs of students share their sentences with the whole group.

Apply

9. Remind students to think about how the words they choose create a mental image for the reader. Today they will write on a topic they choose to improve their writing using adjectives.

Write/Conference

10. Provide time for students to write. After you have scanned for potential confusions, rotate among students and confer with individuals or small groups. It is important to pull in at-risk groups once your students are focused and sustained. Use your Conferring Notebook to keep observations.

Spotlight Strategy

11. Spotlight great adjective use. For example, "Now you've got it! Listen to the extraordinary adjectives used by Shani. You're making it all happen."

Share

12. Have students meet in triads. Then, choose three students to share their work with the whole group. Remember to give a compliment and a comment.

Homework

Ask students to make a list of at least ten adjectives they notice in books and on TV. Ask students to be ready to share their lists in Writer's Workshop tomorrow.

Show Me: Using Action Words

Standards

- Uses descriptive words to convey basic ideas
- Uses verbs in written compositions

Materials

- Chart paper
- Markers
- *Sample Action Words Anchor Chart* (page 186; actionanchorchart.pdf)

Mentor Texts

- *Little Loon and Papa* by Toni Buzzeo
- *Night in the Country* by Cynthia Rylant
- *The Great Fuzz Frenzy* by Susan S. Crummel and Janet Stevens
- See *Mentor Text List* in Appendix C for other suggestions.

Procedures

Note: A fun activity is to take photos of students engaging in different actions. Print the photos and use them to create an action book. Under each photo, the class can come up with a sentence. For example, *Callie climbs on the jungle gym.* Allow students to use the book as a writing resource.

Think About Writing

1. Tell students that writers use a variety of words to show their readers exactly what the characters are doing in their stories.

2. Review a mentor text if desired, and emphasize the action words in it. For example, ask students to listen for the action words author Toni Buzzeo uses to show the actions of Little Loon. Some interesting action words include: *quiver, wobble, squeeze, tuck, zip,* and *dip*.

Teach

3. Tell students, "Today I will show you how to think about actions that can help your readers know more about your story."

4. Create an anchor chart titled *Kids Can*. Write the word *clap* on the chart. Ask students to demonstrate clapping. Tell students the word *clap* is an action word; it is something kids can do. Suggest several other words to add to the chart. Refer to the *Sample Action Words Anchor Chart* (page 186) for examples.

5. Encourage students to think of things kids can do. Have students act out the words and add the words to the chart. Remind students these are all words they can use when writing stories that will help their readers understand their story.

6. Create a story on chart paper about something kids can do using many of the action words from the anchor chart. Either model your thought process as you create the story or have students help write the story.

Show Me: Using Action Words (cont.)

Engage

7. Have students *Heads-up, Stand-up, Partner-up* and work with partners to think of some of the action words they will use in their writing. Encourage them to think of their own or to use the anchor chart as a resource.

Apply

8. Remind students to use action words that help readers know more about the stories they write. Encourage them to use the action words from the anchor chart in their writings.

Write/Conference

9. Provide time for students to write about a topic of their choice. Remember to scan your class for understanding and then begin individual conferences. Ask questions such as, "What are you working on as a writer today? Can you use an action word to tell more about what your character is doing?"

Spotlight Strategy

10. Spotlight effective adjective use. For example, "David is using some outstanding action words in his writing. You're incredible! Good writers use action words to show their readers what is happening in their stories."

Share

11. Have students meet with partners to share their stories. Encourage students to listen for the action words in their partner's writing.

Homework

Ask students to listen for action words they can use in writing. Have students make lists with at least ten action words in them.

Sample Action Words Anchor Chart

Kids can...

- walk
- run
- jump
- hop
- skip
- crawl
- eat
- sleep
- talk

- cry
- laugh
- spell
- sing
- read
- write
- draw
- color
- paint

- smile
- ride
- swim
- splash
- dive
- shout
- dance
- play
- share

#50915—Core of Writing—Level 1   © Shell Education

Amazing Words

Standards

- Uses descriptive words to convey basic ideas
- Uses writing and other methods to describe familiar persons, places, objects, or experiences

Materials

- A mentor text with rich vocabulary
- Chart paper
- Markers
- *My Amazing Words* (page 189; myamazingwords.pdf)

Mentor Texts

- *Fancy Nancy's Favorite Fancy Words* by Jane O'Connor
- *Lily's Purple Plastic Purse* by Kevin Henkes
- *Tough Boris* by Mem Fox
- *The Snowy Day* by Ezra Jack Keats
- See *Mentor Text List* in Appendix C for other suggestions.

Procedures

Note: In this mini-lesson you will develop a class list of interesting words and students will also create their own. Have students add their completed *My Amazing Words* (page 189) to their writing folders.

Think About Writing

1. Tell students that authors create interesting sentences by using a variety of words. Explain that authors know how to add just the right words to show the readers their stories.

Teach

2. Tell students, "Today we will continue to look for interesting words to use in our writing."

3. Review a mentor text, and emphasize the interesting words the author uses. For example, in *Fancy Nancy*, the author uses the word *canine* for the word *dog*.

4. Create an anchor chart titled *Amazing Words*. Write the words you discuss with the class on the chart.

Engage

5. Have students *Heads-up, Stand-up, Partner-up* and work with partners to think about other amazing words they would like to add to the anchor chart. Provide approximately two minutes for students to talk.

6. Allow partners to share the words they discussed. Add the words to the anchor chart. Tell students more words can be added to the anchor chart as they discover new words.

Amazing Words *(cont.)*

Apply

7. Remind students that words are unique or special and add excitement to their writing. Tell students they may wish to spend their writing time today looking at writing they have been working on and revising it by replacing an ordinary word with one from the anchor chart.

Write/Conference

8. Distribute *My Amazing Words* to students. Provide time for students to write their lists. Confer with individuals or small groups. Remember to give a compliment and select a teaching point that the writer can use in future pieces. As you confer today, notice the word choice of your students' writing. Make notes in your Conferring Notebook.

Spotlight Strategy

9. Spotlight amazing word usage. For example, "Jenny is using amazing words in her writing. Outstanding work!" Share the students' sentences with the group.

Share

10. Have students meet with partners to share their work. Ask students to listen for amazing words in their partner's writing.

11. Gather students back together, and have students share any amazing words they heard their partners use. Add the words to the anchor chart.

Homework

Ask students to listen for amazing words they can use in their writing. Have students make lists of at least ten amazing words they would like to use in their writing tomorrow.

Name: _____ Date: _____

My Amazing Words

Directions: Make a list of the amazing words that you know.

_____

_____

_____

_____

_____

_____

_____

_____

_____

Transition Words

Standards

- Uses descriptive words to convey basic ideas
- Uses writing and other methods to describe familiar persons, places, objects, or experiences

Materials

- *Transition Words Cards* (page 192; transitionwordscards.pdf)
- *Sequencing Picture Cards* (pages 193–194; sequencingcards.pdf)

Mentor Texts

- *Pet Show!* by Ezra Jack Keats
- Fairy tales
- Nursery rhymes
- See *Mentor Text List* in Appendix C for other suggestions.

Procedures

Note: Two sets of sequencing cards are provided with this lesson. Choose one or both depending on need. Review the concept of sequencing and transition words. Note transition words as you read them in other mentor texts throughout the year. Create a *Transition Words* anchor chart that can be added to as you encounter them.

Think About Writing

1. Explain to students that good writers sometimes use signal words to tell the reader what is coming next in their writing. They place the words in just the right place so their words flow from one idea to the next in a sequence.

2. Review a mentor text if desired, and emphasize the transition words the author uses.

Teach

3. Tell students, "Today I will show you how to use writing signals to sequence and focus your ideas for your reader."

4. Distribute the *Transition Words Cards* (page 192) to students. Discuss the order noting that *next* and *then* can be used interchangeably.

5. Distribute the cards from the first sheet of *Sequencing Picture Cards* (pages 193) to retell the story of *The Three Bears*. Connect the transition words to the pictures, and retell the story as you really emphasize the transition words.

Engage

6. Distribute the cards from the second sheet of *Sequencing Picture Cards* (pages 194) for the growth of a flower. Have students *Heads-up, Stand-up, Partner-up* and work with partners to use transition words to retell the sequence. Allow time for partners to practice.

Transition Words (cont.)

7. Gather students back together, and have one or two groups share the story out loud.

Apply

8. Remind students to use transition words in their writing piece today where it is appropriate to help the reader understand the sequence of their stories.

Write/Conference

9. Provide time for students to write. As you work with students, keep in mind that it takes time and practice for students to effectively use transition words. You may attend to a small group or individually confer. Remember to jot down your observations.

Spotlight Strategy

10. Spotlight students using transition words well. For example, "Tatiana is signaling to her reader that she is moving into a new thought! Great job, Tatiana!"

Share

11. Have students meet in triads to share their writing. Ask students to share any transition words they used in their writing. Provide approximately two minutes.

Homework

Ask students to write a few sentences using transition words about something they did today.

Transition Words Cards

Teacher Directions: Cut out the cards below and display them for students. Model how to create a sentence using *Transition Words Cards* to describe the sequence of events on the *Sequencing Picture Cards* (pages 193–194).

First | Then

Next | Finally

#50915—Core of Writing—Level 1

Sequencing Picture Cards

Teacher Directions: Cut out the cards below and have students determine the sequence of events using transition words.

Sequencing Picture Cards (cont.)

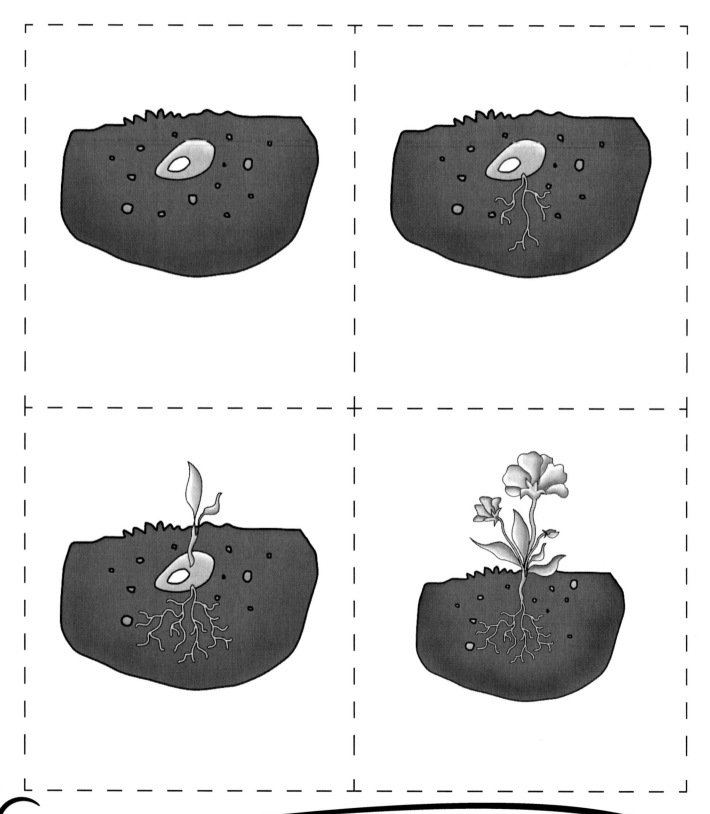

#50915—Core of Writing—Level 1

Sounds All Around from A to Z

Standards

- Uses descriptive words to convey basic ideas
- Uses writing and other methods to describe familiar persons, places, objects, or experiences

Materials

- *Onomatopoeia Dictionary* (pages 197–202; onomatopoeiadic.pdf)
- *Teacher Resources for Onomatopoeia* (pages 203–204; teacheronomatopoeia.pdf) *(optional)*
- Chart paper
- Markers

Mentor Texts

- *Bear Snores On* by Karma Wilson
- *Night in the Country* by Cynthia Rylant
- *Click, Clack, Moo* and *Giggle, Giggle, Quack* Doreen Cronin
- See *Mentor Text List* in Appendix C for other suggestions.

Procedures

Note: You may wish to create the booklet on one day and revisit it the next day to share additional text, and encourage writers to use the words in their own writing. Use the *Teacher Resources for Onomatopoeia* (pages 203–204) for additional words, ideas, and texts to teach this lesson.

Think About Writing

1. Explain to students that authors add just the right words to their writing so the reader can create a mental image of their stories. Good writers also want their reader to hear what is happening in their stories. One way they accomplish that task is by using a special writing tool called *onomatopoeia*. Have students repeat the word several times in different ways such as by slightly separating syllables or by snapping the beat.

Teach

2. Tell students, "Today I will show you how to use *onomatopoeia* in your writing." Explain that *onomatopoeia* is the use of words that sound just like the noise or action they are describing, like the sounds that animals make: *moo, baa, quack* or noise words like: *drip, pop,* and *sizzle.* These are the sounds all around us that we hear every day.

3. Review a mentor text and ask students to find a few examples of words that represent onomatopoeia.

4. Write the word *onomatopoeia* on a sheet of chart paper. Think aloud as you recall and record any sound words from the mentor text on the chart.

Engage

5. Continue reading from a mentor text. Ask students to *Heads-up, Stand-up, Partner-up* and work with partners to listen for any additional use of *onomatopoeia.* Have students count on their fingers the words they find.

Sounds All Around from A to Z *(cont.)*

6. Read the text a few pages at a time. Stop and have partners *Turn and Talk* about the words they heard from the story. Have students share the words with the whole group and record the words on the anchor chart.

7. Tell students more words can be added to the anchor chart throughout the year as they encounter them in reading, writing, and listening.

Apply

8. Remind students to use words that help their readers hear what is happening in their writing, just like the mentor text author. Provide students with the pages for the *Onomatopoeia Dictionary* (pages 197–202). Tell students to work with partners to assemble the pages and discuss other words to add to the dictionary. Have students store the dictionary in their writing folders to use as a resource when they are writing. Tell students they can add new words from the anchor chart that they may want to include in their own writing.

Write/Conference

9. Provide time for students to write in their *Onomatopoeia Dictionary*. Monitor, support, and provide positive feedback as you rotate among students to confer.

Spotlight Strategy

10. Spotlight students that are working together efficiently and with a strong work ethic. Notice students that may be discussing other words to add to their booklet.

Share

11. Have the partners who worked together to create the dictionary meet up with another pair to create quads. Ask students to share their dictionaries and discuss the onomatopoeia words they included and how they plan to use them in writing.

Homework

Ask students to listen for sound words all around them this evening. Have students make a list of at least five sound words.

Onomatopoeia Dictionary

Teacher Directions: Cut out the pages for students and staple them in ABC order. Have students add new words to their dictionaries as they learn them.

My Onomatopoeia Dictionary

Sounds All Around from A–Z

Name: _____

A is for... achoo

B is for... beep

C is for... crunch

Onomatopoeia Dictionary *(cont.)*

D is for...
ding

E is for...
eek

F is for...
fizz

G is for...
gasp

Onomatopoeia Dictionary *(cont.)*

H is for...
hum

I is for...
itch

J is for...
jangle

K is for...
knock knock

Onomatopoeia Dictionary *(cont.)*

L is for...
la

M is for...
mumble

N is for...
neigh

O is for...
ouch

Onomatopoeia Dictionary *(cont.)*

P is for...
puff

Q is for...
quack

R is for...
rumble

S is for...
splash

Onomatopoeia Dictionary *(cont.)*

T is for...
tap tap

U and **V**
are for...
ugh   vroom

W is for...
whoosh

Y and **Z** are
for...
yikes   zonk

Teacher Resources for Onomatopoeia

A	C	E	I	P	S	U
achoo	chatter	eeek	icky	phew	screech	ugh
ahem	cheep		itch	ping	shuffle	
	chirp	**F**		plop	shush	**V**
B	chomp	fizz	**J**	plunk	sizzle	vroom
baa	choo, choo	flick	jangle	poof	slam	
bah	clang	flutter	jingle	pop	slap	**W**
bam	clank			puff	slash	whack
bang	clap	**G**	**K**	purr	slurp	wham
bark	clatter	gasp	knock-knock		smack	whip
bash	click	giggle		**Q**	snap	whisper
bawl	clink	growl	**L**	quack	sniff	whizz
beep	cluck	gr-r-r-r	la		snip	whoop
belch	clunk	grunt		**R**	snort	whoosh
blare	coo	gurgle	**M**	Rat-a-tat-tat	splash	woof
blurt	crack		meow	rattle	squelch	whirl
boing	crackle		moo	rev	squish	
boink	crunch	**H**	mumble	ring	stomp	
bong	cuckoo	hack	murmur	roar	swirl	
bonk		hiccup		rumble	swish	**X**
boo	**D**	hiss	**N**	rustle	swoosh	
boom	ding	honk	neigh			
bow-wow	drip	hoot			**T**	**Y**
bubble	drop	howl	**O**		thud	yo-yo
bump		huh	oink		thump	
buzz		hum	ouch		tick-tock	**Z**
			ow		tinkle	zap
					tsk	zing
					twang	zip
					tweet	zoom
					twirl	

Teacher Resources for Onomatopoeia (cont.)

Game—What's That Sound?

Provide students with a sound and have students name the source. For example, say, "Moo," and students should respond, "Cow." Another way to play would be to show them a card with the picture of the object making noise. For more advanced students, write the word and have them analyze and find the appropriate noise. The game can also be played by having the teacher name the source and students name the sound. Examples include: *cat, duck, dog, sheep, snake, train, balloon, ocean, door, wind, storm, fireworks, phone,* etc.

Additional Mentor Texts Containing Onomatopoeia

- *Achoo! Bang! Crash! The Noisy Alphabet* by Ross MacDonald
- *Zoom Broom* by Margie Palatini
- *The Little Old Lady Who Was Not Afraid of Anything* by Linda D. Willams and Megan Lloyd
- *The Little Mouse, The Red Strawberry, and The BIG Hungry Bear* by Audrey Wood

Voice

Expressing Yourself

Voice is evident in the stories and literature we share with our students every day. It is in those books that we can barely tear ourselves away from, the ones we want to keep reading and can hardly wait to turn the page. Think about the texts you pull out to read to your students again and again. You want to share them because the author's voice connects in some way to you personally. To call attention to voice, collect examples on anchor charts, help students recognize and value its purpose through your read alouds and student writing, and model writing with differing emotions. Sprinkle your comments in spotlighting with comments like, "Notice the way Jesse described what happened after dinner so that you felt you were in the moment with him." "I love the way Josh made his writing sound just like his talking."

Voice is what makes writing come alive. It is the personality of the writer coming through in the writing. Although sometimes difficult to teach, it is recognizable in writing through the personal tone and feeling of the writing piece. This section contains lessons that focus on how students can connect with their readers to compel them to continue reading. This section includes the following:

- Lesson 1: *More Than Happy, Sad, and Mad* (page 207)

- Lesson 2: *Voice Times Two* (page 210)

Introduce the *Val and Van Voice* poster (page 206) during the first lesson on voice. It can be displayed in the room to provide a visual reminder for students that *Voice* is one of the traits of writing. Then, refer to the poster when teaching other lessons on voice.

Val and Van Voice

What is the purpose of my writing?

✔ Did I write to an audience?

✔ Did I share my feelings?

✔ Did I make my reader smile, cry, think?

✔ Does my writing sound like me?

More Than Happy, Sad, and Mad

Standard

Writes expressive compositions (uses an individual, authentic voice)

Materials

- Chart paper
- Markers
- *My Feelings* (page 209; myfeelings.pdf)

Mentor Texts

- *On Monday When It Rained* by Cherryl Kachenmeister
- *Chrysanthemum* by Kevin Henkes
- See *Mentor Text List* in Appendix C for other suggestions.

Procedures

Note: This mini-lesson may be revisited by adding additional feeling words to the anchor chart for writing support.

Think About Writing

1. Explain to students that authors use specific details and just the right words to tell their amazing stories. Brilliant authors also use a bit of magic called *voice*. Voice is what makes us laugh out loud or feel unhappy. In the story *The Three Little Pigs*, voice is what shows us the pigs are frightened and we should be afraid of the wolf. Voice shows up in writing in many different ways and one way is through using feelings or emotions in our writing.

2. Review a mentor text if desired, and emphasize the author's use of voice. Discuss the feelings related to the character.

Teach

3. Tell students, "Today I will show you how to explore how to use your feelings to tell stories more clearly." Explain that beginning writers sometimes use the same words in their writing. For example, "It was sad," or "I was happy." But, those words do not give the reader enough information.

4. Ask students to identify words that tell about feelings. Create an anchor chart of the words. Illustrate a face next to each word to add picture support. Another idea is to use a digital camera to take pictures of children making faces to show different emotions. Post the photographs next to the corresponding words on the anchor chart.

More Than Happy, Sad, and Mad *(cont.)*

5. Model how to emulate a mentor text author's voice as you write your own story. For example, tell students, "In *On Monday When It Rained*, the author uses a pattern to tell her story. Tell students, "Today, we will use our own pattern to create our own stories. First, I will pick a day of the week: *Thursday*. Then, I will pick my feeling word: *worried*. Now, what would make me worried: bad weather, my kitten, a sick friend? So I will pick just one and complete my story. *On Thursday, my kitten did not come home. I was worried.*"

Engage

6. Have partners *Heads-up, Stand-up, Partner-up* and work together to identify the feeling they will describe in their writing today. Encourage partners to ask each other what made them feel that way. Allow time for discussion.

Apply

7. Remind students that there are many feelings they can use in their writing. Distribute *My Feelings* (page 209) and have students use the template to frame their writing. Encourage students to use the anchor chart to find words that tell more than *happy*, *sad*, and *mad*.

Write/Conference

8. Provide time for students to write. Scan for and resolve any confusion. Confer with students individually or in small groups. Make observations in your Conferring Notebook.

Spotlight Strategy

9. Spotlight a student who shows great emotion in their writing. For example, "Jesse made decisions quickly and is using details to show his emotion. Amazing writing work today!"

Share

10. Have students come to the Author's Chair and share their writing. Remember to provide lots of affirmation.

Homework

Ask students to listen for voice in stories they hear from books or on TV. Remind them that voice is the magic that makes us laugh, shiver, or even cry.

Name: _____ Date: _____

My Feelings

Directions: Complete the sentences to tell about a feeling you have had. Then, draw a picture of your story.

On _____,

(day of the week)

_____

_____

I was _____.

(feeling word)

Voice Times Two

Standard

Writes expressive compositions (uses an individual, authentic voice)

Materials

- Chart paper
- Markers
- Writing paper

Mentor Texts

- *I Am the Dog, I Am the Cat* by Donald Hall
- *No, David!* by David Shannon
- See *Mentor Text List* in Appendix C for other suggestions.

Procedures

Note: This mini-lesson lends itself to two-voice poetry and is a fun Author's Tea activity or class book.

Think About Writing

1. Remind students that authors build sentences and select just the right words to make their writing more interesting for the reader. Tell students that another way to interest readers is with the writing trait of *voice*. Authors use expressions and feelings of their characters, along with illustrations, to make their stories memorable for their readers.

2. Review a mentor text if desired, and emphasize the author's use of voice. Have students listen for the way the author uses characters, their feelings, and the illustrations to show voice. For example, in *No, David!*, David Shannon makes us want to hurry and turn the page to find out what David will do next.

Teach

3. Tell students, "Today I will show you how to use voice in your writing to show your reader what your characters are thinking and feeling."

4. Model for students how to show voice for two different characters: a dad and a child. Create a two-column chart with the characters listed at the top of each column. Develop a few ideas for the characters. For example:

Dad	Child
Go fishing	Play
Watch sports	Ride a bike
Eat steak and potatoes	Play video games
	Watch cartoons
	Eat pizza

Voice Times Two *(cont.)*

5. Fold a sheet of writing paper in half. On one half write from a dad's perspective. On the other half, write from a child's perspective. Model writing with voice through your word choice and in the illustrations. For example, show emotions on the faces of the characters or add speech bubbles. To extend the lesson, have students make a booklet using paper folded in half. Have them select two characters to show perspective. Suggested character pairs include: pigs/wolf, goldilocks/bears, boy/girl, boy/ant, flower/bee, and mouse/rat.

Engage

6. Have students *Heads-up, Stand-up, Partner-up* and work with partners to discuss characters they may use in their writing. Allow time for discussion. Then have students share their ideas with the whole group. List students' ideas on chart paper for them to reference as they write.

Apply

7. Remind students that they can give their stories voice by showing their character's feelings, emotions, and attitudes both in their word choice and illustrations.

Write/Conference

8. Provide time for students to write. Scan for and resolve any confusion. Confer with students individually or in small groups, making observations in your Conferring Notebook.

Spotlight Strategy

9. Spotlight great use of voice. For example, "Listen to the way Makala has added voice to her writing. I know right away her character is angry. Outstanding writing work!"

Share

10. Have students meet with partners to share their writing. Ask partners to listen carefully to see if they can tell what the character is feeling.

Homework

Ask students to write down the titles of three books from home or the library where they hear clear examples of voice from the author.

Conventions
Checking Your Writing

Writing that does not follow standard conventions is difficult to read. The use of correct capitalization, punctuation, spelling, and grammar is what makes writing consistent and easy to read. Students need to have reasonable control over the conventions of writing. This section provides lessons that guide students to internalize conventions as they write and as they check their work after they have written a piece. Lessons in this section include the following:

- Lesson 1: Using the Alphabet Chart (page 215)
- Lesson 2: The Capital Rap (page 218)
- Lesson 3: Using the Vowel Chart (page 221)
- Lesson 4: Hear It! Say It! Sound Boxes (page 226)
- Lesson 5: Movin' to Edit (page 230)
- Lesson 6: Using the Digraphs and Blends Chart (page 233)
- Lesson 7: My Writing Checklist (page 237)
- Lesson 8: Perfect Punctuation (page 240)
- Lesson 9: My Editing Guide (page 243)

The *Callie, Super Conventions Checker* poster (page 214) can be displayed in the room to provide a visual reminder for students that conventions are one of the traits of writing. Introduce this poster during the first lesson on conventions. Refer to the poster when teaching other lessons on conventions to refresh students' memories.

Callie
Super Conventions Checker

How do I edit my paper?

✓ Did I check my capitalization?

✓ Did I check my punctuation?

✓ Did I check my spelling?

✓ Did I use good spacing?

✓ Did I read over my story?

#50915—Core of Writing—Level 1   © Shell Education

Using the Alphabet Chart

Standard
Uses conventions of spelling in written compositions

Materials
- Chart paper
- Markers
- *Alphabet Chart* (page 217; alphabetchart.pdf)

Mentor Text
- *Alphabet Mystery* by Audrey and Bruce Wood
- *A, My Name is Alice* by Jane E. Bayer
- See *Mentor Text List* in Appendix C for other suggestions.

Procedures
Note: Use the *Alphabet Chart* (page 217) or any other your school or district may have available.

Think About Writing
1. Tell students that authors use letters and sounds to make words that we can read. Readers and writers use many resources (tools) to assist them in their writing efforts. Explain to students that alphabet charts are used until they no longer need them to write words that are needed for stories.

2. Review a mentor text if desired, and emphasize the organization as an alphabet book.

Teach
3. Tell students, "Today I will show you how to use an alphabet chart to spell words you are unsure about." Display the *Alphabet Chart* and review the letters and pictures.

4. Think aloud as you model using the chart. For example, "My story will say, 'I can hop.' I will say the word *can* slowly so that I can hear the beginning sound /c/. Next I will move to my chart and see if I can find a picture of something that begins with /c/. Yes, I see that cat starts with the same sound, so I will write that letter. Next, I will do the best I can for the rest of the word and other words in my story." Continue modeling with the remainder of the sentence. Add additional words based on student needs.

Using the Alphabet Chart (cont.)

Engage

5. Ask students to think about how they might use the *Alphabet Chart* to help them write new words. Have students *Turn and Talk* with partners about what they will write today and how they might use this chart. Alphabet charts should be available for student use throughout the day. These charts can be laminated and placed on the table during writing time or kept permanently in student writing folders.

Apply

6. Remind students to use the *Alphabet Chart* to help them write words that are needed to create their messages.

Write/Conference

7. Provide time for students to write. Scan the group to assure that all students are engaged. Then rotate around the room and begin individual or small group discussions with students. Remember to record observations in the Conferring Notebook.

Spotlight Strategy

8. Spotlight successful student work. For example, "Charlotte has her alphabet chart placed in a special place so that she can use it as needed. Really smart thinking! I love the way you're always thinking about your important writing work."

Share

9. Have students meet in groups of three (triads) to share their writing. Remind students to pay a compliment or give praise. Provide approximately two minutes for students to talk.

Homework

Ask students to make a list of the alphabet and to write one word that begins with each letter.

Alphabet Chart

A a	B b	C c	D d	E e
apple	ball	cat	dog	elephant
F f	**G g**	**H h**	**I i**	**J j**
fish	gorilla	hat	igloo	jump rope
K k	**L l**	**M m**	**N n**	**O o**
kite	lion	monkey	nuts	octopus
P p	**Q q**	**R r**	**S s**	**T t**
pig	queen	rabbit	socks	tent
U u	**V v**	**W w**	**X x**	**Y y**
umbrella	vacuum	wagon	X-ray	yo-yo
				Z z
				zipper

The Capital Rap

Standards

- Uses strategies to edit and publish written work
- Uses conventions of capitalization in written compositions

Materials

- *Capital Rap* (page 220; capitalrap.pdf)
- Chart paper
- Markers

Mentor Texts

- *One Monday Morning* by Uri Shulevitz
- *I Like Myself!* by Karen Beaumont
- See *Mentor Text List* in Appendix C for other suggestions.

Procedures

Note: Teach this lesson over several days and revisit it regularly until students have perfected the skill of capitalization. You may wish to introduce one section of the *Capital Rap* (page 220) and focus on those specific concepts before moving onto the next section.

Think About Writing

1. Explain to students that authors need to use punctuation correctly so that the reader understands the message.

2. Review a mentor text if desired, and emphasize the author's use of capitalization. For example, in *I Like Myself!*, author Karen Beaumont is like a busy bee. She flies around on almost every page using the word *I* to begin many sentences. Every sentence in her book begins with a capital letter. In *One Monday Morning,* Uri Shulevitz uses days of the week to sequence his story. Remind students that they should try to immitate the authors they love as they work on writing projects.

Teach

3. Tell students, "Today I will show you how to use a rap to remember capitalization."

4. Teach students the *Capital Rap*.

   - Use a soft voice and snap fingers to the beat, "I am important, So are you, The beginning of a sentence is important too."

   - Have students join in as you point to the words and repeat several times.

The Capital Rap (cont.)

- Write the example sentences on chart paper and emphasize the capitalization rule as you correct the sentences with students.

  Richard and i are friends.
  (capitalize *I*)

  mrs. gaston is our teacher.
  (capitalize a person's name)

  we like to write and read stories.
  (capitalize the first letter of a sentence)

5. Remind students they can use *Capital Rap* quietly while they work to edit their writing pieces.

Engage

6. Have students *Heads-up, Stand-up, Partner-up* and work with partners to repeat the *Capital Rap* using a soft voice and snapping fingers. Then have partners explain to each other in their own words exactly what the rap is reminding them to do. Encourage students to take turns. Provide approximately two minutes of talk time.

Apply

7. Remind students to use the conventions of print—capitalization, punctuation, and spelling—to make their message clear for the reader. Encourage students to work on a piece of writing from their folders or begin a new piece as they work today.

Write/Conference

8. Provide time for students to write. Be ready to jot down what you notice about students' writing to plan your next instruction.

Spotlight Strategy

9. Invite your students to spotlight someone's work. For example, "You are all doing such important work. Does anyone have a spotlight they would like to share? You all did a fantastic job remembering and using the *Capital Rap!*"

Share

10. Have students meet with partners to share the work they did today. Ask students to look for correct capitalization in their partners' work. Remind them to compliment each other and ask meaningful questions about each other's writing.

Homework

Have students take home a copy of the *Capital Rap* and share it with their parents. Have them practice the rap at home this evening.

Capital Rap

Teacher Directions: Teach students to sing the rap in a soft voice as they snap to the beat. Review the examples of capitalization as you teach each verse of *Capital Rap*.

Rap	Examples

Capital Rap, Capital Rap
I am important.
So are you.
The beginning of a sentence
Is important too.
Capital Rap, Capital Rap
	Capitalize the word *I*.
	    Richard and **I** are friends.
	Capitalize a person's name.
	    Mrs. Gaston is our teacher.
	Capitalize the first letter in a sentence.
	    We like to write and read stories.

Capital Rap, Capital Rap
Days of the week
and months of the year,
Cities and states
Need capitals it's clear!
Capital Rap, Capital Rap
	Capitalize the days of the week.
	    Today is **Saturday**!
	Capitalize the months of the year.
	    My birthday is in **April**.
	Capitalize the names of cities and states.
	    I live in **Chicago, Illinois**.

Capital Rap, Capital Rap
Titles of a book,
Movie or TV,
A special place and holiday
Need capitals, you see!
Capital Rap, Capital Rap
	Capitalize the important words in a title.
	    I read "**The Princess and the Pea**."
	Capitalize the names of special places.
	    My family went to **Disneyland**.
	Capitalize names of holidays.
	    We have a picnic on the **Fourth of July**.

Using the Vowel Chart

Standard

Uses conventions of spelling in written compositions

Materials

• *Vowel Word List* (page 225; vowelwordlist.pdf)
• *Vowel Chart* (pages 223–224; vowelchart.pdf)

Mentor Texts

• *The Fat Cat Sat on the Mat* by Nurit Karling
• *Little Red Hen* by Paul Galdone
• *Whistle for Willie* by Ezra Jack Keats
• See *Mentor Text List* in Appendix C for other suggestions.

Procedures

Note: Repeat this lesson on vowel sounds as needed throughout the year. See *Vowel Word List* (page 225) for additional words.

Think About Writing

1. Explain that five letters of the alphabet do more than the rest of the letters combined. Those letters are called *vowels* and they are *a*, *e*, *i*, *o*, and *u*. Teach students a cheer. For example, "Give me an *a*." Then say the short vowel sound for *a* three times: /a/, /a/, /a/. Have students say the letter name with their fists up in the air. Then have them repeat the sound three times: /a/, /a/, /a/. Repeat this with each short vowel. Use this activity with other sounds, including the long vowel sounds.

Teach

2. Tell students, "Today I will show you how to use a vowel chart to listen for target sounds." Display the *Vowel Chart* (pages 223–224) and tell students that they will practice using the chart to listen for target sounds.

3. Tell students you will say a word slowly, for example, the word *cat*. Model for students how to use your hand to segment a word (you are modeling a mirror image so they will use the oppostite hands):

   • Open your right hand off to the side for the initial sound /c/.
   • Make a fist with your left hand and punch up in the air three times as you say the vowel: /a/, /a/, /a/.
   • Open the left hand for the ending sound /t/.
   • Bring fists together and say the word *cat*.

   Locate the /a/ sound on the *Vowel Chart* and point out the letter *a* that makes the /a/ sound in words. Tell students that this is the letter they will use for /a/. Model a few additional words for students. Words can be taken out of a mentor text if desired.

Using the Vowel Chart *(cont.)*

Engage

4. Have students *Heads-up, Stand-up, Partner-up* and sit next to partners (to avoid confusion) to identify the vowel sounds in words. Tell students you will say a word. Ask one partner to say the word and the sounds as he or she uses hand motions to spell the word.

5. Continue practicing with additional words. Have partners switch roles so that they have practice in each role.

Apply

6. Distribute the *Vowel Chart* to students. Have them keep it in their writing folders as a writing tool. Explain to students that authors use tools to help write specific and accurate words to express their thoughts and ideas; they do not just write words that they know. Remind students to use the many tools they are gathering in their writing folders to help them as they write.

Write/Conference

7. Provide time for students to write. Take a moment to scan your class and see if anyone is having difficulty getting started. Immediately take care of those needs; then begin to confer with individuals or small groups to enrich or reteach.

Spotlight Strategy

8. Spotlight someone who is using the vowel chart effectively. For example, "Writers, you're the best! Faraz is a shining star for trying to say words slowly and using the vowel chart writing tool. Great listening!"

Share

9. Have students meet with partners to share the writing they did today. Remind students to give a compliment and ask a question about their partner's writing.

Homework

Ask students to make a list of the vowels. Have them write at least two words for each letter that contain the vowel sound. Tell them there will be a chart and marker by the door tomorrow. They can add any words they have found to the chart.

Name: _____ Date: _____

Vowel Chart

Short Vowels				
a	e	i	o	u
apple	elephant	igloo	octopus	umbrella
cat	bed	pig	dog	sun

Vowel Chart (cont.)

Long Vowels				
—a	e	i	o	u
apron	**e**agle	**i**ce cream	**o**val	**u**niform
c**a**ke	b**ee**	b**i**ke	b**o**ne	c**u**be

#50915—Core of Writing—Level 1

Vowel Word List

Short A	Short E	Short I	Short O	Short U
add	bed	big	box	bug
ant	beg	did	dog	bus
apple	egg	dig	dot	but
ax	elk	drip	fox	drum
cat	elm	fish	frog	fun
dad	get	fit	hop	gum
fast	hen	inch	hot	hug
flag	leg	ink	log	hum
glad	men	kid	mom	rub
had	nest	lid	not	rug
man	pet	lip	on	run
pan	red	milk	pop	sun
rat	sled	mix	sock	tub
sad	ten	pig	stop	up
tag	wet	sit	top	us

Short/Long A	Short/Long E	Short/Long I	Short/Long O	Short/Long U
can/cane	pet/Pete	dim/dime	cop/cope	cub/cube
cap/cape		fin/fine	glob/globe	cut/cute
fad/fade		kit/kite	hop/hope	hug/huge
hat/hate		rid/ride	pop/pope	tub/tube
mad/made		rip/ripe	slop/slope	
pal/pale		slid/slide		
Sam/same		slim/slime		
tap/tape		Tim/time		
		twin/twine		
		fin/fine		

Long A	Long E	Long I	Long O	Long U
ape	feet	dime	bone	cute
cake	he	ice	broke	flute
date	me	like	cone	fuse
face	see	shine	drove	June
grapes	she	side	rope	rude
make	tree	size	smoke	rule
shake	bee	smile	stove	tune
skate	we	white	woke	use

Hear It! Say It! Sound Boxes

Standard

Uses conventions of spelling in written compositions

Materials

- Place markers
- *Hear It! Say It! Sound Boxes* (page 228; hearsaysoundboxes.pdf)
- *Hear It! Say It! Sound Box Word List* (page 229; hearsaysoundwordlist.pdf)

Mentor Texts

- *The Cat in the Hat* by Dr. Seuss
- See *Mentor Text List* in Appendix C for other suggestions.

Procedures

Note: The goal for students is to gain automaticity with two to five phonemes. Providing support early builds a strong sound/symbol match to problem solve difficult words. Start simple and move to more complex words. Adapted from Elkonin (1973).

Think About Writing

1. Explain to students that authors use many resources to write words correctly. Tell students that knowing the right letters and sounds to use in words will help them write their stories more quickly. Explain that when they struggle to write the words, they sometimes forget what they wanted to say.

2. Tell students that using sound boxes will give them more confidence. Explain that they will learn to separate words into sounds to quickly problem solve tricky words.

Teach

3. Tell students, "Today I will show you how to use sound boxes to support your word writing."

4. Model for students how to say the sounds in a word. Display *Hear It! Say It! Sound Boxes* (page 228) activity sheet so they can easily watch your demonstration.

5. Say a word, for example, *at*. Say each sound in the word. As you say each sound, push a place marker into a box. For example, say /a/ and push a place marker into the first box. Then say /t/ and push a place marker into the second box.

6. Demonstrate how to use each of the boxes on the activity sheet for longer words. Remind students they will use two boxes when there are two sounds like in *at*, three boxes for words with three sounds, like *cat*, and so on.

Hear It! Say It! Sound Boxes (cont.)

Engage

7. Have students return to their desks with a copy of *Hear It! Say It! Sound Boxes.* Provide place markers to groups. Review with students the purpose of the place markers so they understand that they markers are a writing tool and not for play.

8. Use words from *Hear It! Say It! Sound Box Word List* (page 229) or a mentor text with students as they practice. Use the following explicit instructions:

- Say the word.
- Repeat the word once.
- Move the place markers into the boxes as you say each sound.
- Slide your fingers rapidly under the word as you say it quickly.

Remind students to support each other as they practice.

9. Practice with several words. Remember to begin with words with two sounds and then proceed with longer words as students are ready for words with more sounds.

Apply

10. Encourage students to use *Hear It! Say It! Sound Boxes* for support as they write their stories.

Write/Conference

11. Provide time for students to write. Then rotate around the room to confer with students and make observations.

Spotlight Strategy

12. Spotlight a student using the strategy and share it with the whole group.

Share

13. Have students *Turn and Talk* to partners to share several words they tried to write using the sound boxes. Provide approximately two minutes for students to talk.

Homework
Ask students to make lists of at least five words that have two sounds (or whatever number of sounds you practiced).

Name: _____ Date: _____

Hear It! Say It! Sound Boxes

Directions: Push a place holder into each box for each sound you hear.

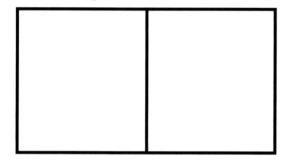

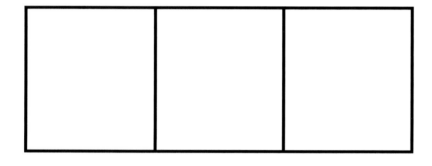

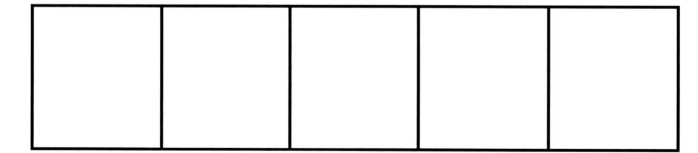

#50915—Core of Writing—Level 1   © Shell Education

Hear It! Say It!
Sound Box Word List

2 Phonemes	3 Phonemes	4 Phonemes	5 Phonemes
am	bed	best	blend
at	beg	black	cradle
boo	big	brown	crunch
bow	boat	bump	grand
day	bus	clap	plant
egg	cub	crab	pleased
go	cup	dress	plump
if	fall	dump	scrape
is	hop	fast	scream
it	house	glad	slept
me	job	grape	spend
my	man	green	splash
see	mouth	left	spread
shoe	over	milk	spring
shy	play	skate	stamp
so	push	stop	stand
toe	shop	swim	stripe
up	sun	think	strong
we	tell	truck	trust
zoo	web	wind	twist

Movin' to Edit

Standards

- Uses strategies to edit and publish written work
- Uses conventions of capitalization in written compositions
- Uses conventions of punctuation in written compositions

Materials

- *Movin' to Edit* (page 232; movintoedit.pdf)
- Sentence Strips
- Markers
- Sticky notes

Mentor Texts

- *Are You My Mother?* by P. D. Eastman
- *No, David!* by David Shannon
- *The Relatives Came* by Cynthia Rylant
- See *Mentor Text List* in Appendix C for other suggestions.

Procedures

Note: Revisit this lesson to practice additional conventions for editing, such as commas and quotation marks.

Think About Writing

1. Explain to students that authors develop interesting sentences in their writing. Authors know that readers must use strategies to understand when one sentence ends and another begins. Good writers know to begin their sentences with a capital letter and end their thoughts with an ending punctuation mark.

2. Review a mentor text if desired, and emphasize how the author uses punctuation to clarify and add energy to his or her writing.

Teach

3. Tell students, "Today I will show you a fun way to remember how sentences begin and end."

4. Write the following sentences on sentence strips:

   - *my name is Vickie*
   - *how old are you*
   - *i am six years old*
   - *my friend is sam*
   - *we like to hike and look for snakes*
   - *eeek*

5. Place the strips in a pocket chart and read the sentences without stopping. Discuss the difficulty of understanding the message of the words.

Movin' to Edit (cont.)

6. Tell students that sometimes we forget to begin a sentence with a capital letter and end it with punctuation. Model using your body as you say the first sentence to help students remember conventions.

   - Stand tall with hands together over head and say the first word in the sentence. *(My)* Tell students this represents a capital letter.

   - Continue saying the rest of the sentence. *(name is Vickie)*

   - Signify the period at the end of the sentence by grinding your right foot into the ground. *(.)*

7. Add sticky notes to the sentence strips to correct them.

8. Continue modeling the remainder of the sentences using body movements to represent conventions. See *Movin' to Edit* (page 232) for body movements that correspond to each convention.

Engage

9. Have students *Heads-up, Stand-up, Partner-up* and work with partners to practice using the body motions to show their understanding of capitals and ending punctuation. Have students practice using the sentence strips. Allow approximately two minutes for student practice. Rove, engage, and support students. Gather students back together and highlight and compliment partners using appropriate behaviors and demonstrating lesson focus.

Apply

10. Remind students they should capitalize the first word in a sentence and finish with ending punctuation to let the reader know when one sentence is finished and another is beginning. Remind students to always check this in their writing!

Write/Conference

11. Provide time for students to write. Observe students to check for understanding. Initiate individual or small group conferences. Take notes in your Conferring Notebook.

Spotlight Strategy

12. Spotlight great editors. For example, "Amee did what good writers do! She capitalized the first word of every sentence and has included punctuation at the end of each."

Share

13. Have students meet with partners to share how they included capitals and punctuation in their writing.

Homework

Ask students to copy two sentences out of books tonight. Remind them to include all the capitalization and punctuation in the sentences.

Movin' to Edit

Capital: Stand tall with hands together overhead

Period: Right foot grinds into floor

Question: Shrug shoulders with hands up

Exclamation: Right arm straight up and down, then punch with left arm

Comma: Right hand karate chop (gently)

Quotation Mark: Bent elbows, slant left and wiggle hands, slant right and wiggle hands

Using the Digraphs and Blends Chart

Standard

Uses conventions of spelling in written compositions

Materials

- Chart paper
- Markers
- *Digraphs and Consonant Blends Sound Chart* (pages 235–236; blendschart.pdf)

Mentor Texts

- *Sheep in a Jeep* by Nancy Shaw
- *A Chair for My Mother* by Vera B. Williams
- *The Frail Snail on the Trail* by Brian Cleary
- See *Mentor Text List* in Appendix C for other suggestions.

Procedure

Note: Students in first grade are still learning to master blends and digraphs. Note which students need additional reteaching in an individual or small group setting.

Think About Writing

1. Explain to students that authors use many tools to write words the reader can read. Tell students that they can use letter/sound charts until they no longer need them to write words.

2. Review a mentor text if desired, and emphasize the author's use of correct spelling.

Teach

3. Tell students, "Today I will show you how to use another tool to help you spell the words you want to write."

4. Display the *Digraphs and Consonant Blends Sound Chart* (pages 235–236) so students can see it. Explain that you will show them how to use it to spell words.

5. Tell students, "My story will say, 'I saw a fly on the door.'" Explain to students you are not sure how to spell *fly*.

   - Model how to say the beginning sound in the word, (/fl/).
   - Tell students to look at the chart and see if there is a picture that begins with /fl/. Point to the flower and emphasize that *flower* starts with the same sound.
   - Model how to write the letters *fl*.
   - Show students how to sound out the rest of the word. Use a sound spelling chart to show that *y* makes the long *i* sound at the end of a word.

   Repeat this procedure with additional sentences and words.

Using the Digraphs and Blends Chart *(cont.)*

Engage

6. Distribute the *Digraphs and Consonant Blends Sound Chart* to students. Say words that have digraphs or consonant blends in them. Have students *Heads-up, Stand-up, Partner-up* and work with partners to identify the spelling of the sounds in the words. Begin with words that have the digraphs and consonant blends at the beginning of the words. Once students are comfortable identifying those sounds, provide them words with the sounds in the middle or the end, for example: **dr**ip, bro**th**er, and mun**ch**.

Apply

7. Remind students to use the digraph and blends chart to help them write words that are needed to create a message. Tell them the digraph and blends chart can be placed in their writing folders as a resource for when they are writing.

Write/Conference

8. Provide time for students to write. Scan your group to assure that all are engaged. Rotate around the room and begin individual or small group discussions with students. Remember to record observations in your Conferring Notebook.

Spotlight Strategy

9. Gather students back together and spotlight student work. For example, "Natalia has her digraph/blends chart in a special place so that she can use it as needed. Really smart thinking! I love the way you're always thinking about your important writing work."

Share

10. Have students meet in triads to share the writing they did today. Remind students to pay a compliment or give praise. Provide approximately two minutes for students to share.

Homework

Ask students to make lists of at least five words with blends or digraphs.

Name: _____ Date: _____

Digraphs and Consonant Blends Sound Chart

sh	ch	th	wh	bl
sheep	**ch**air	**th**umb	**wh**ale	**bl**ocks
cl	fl	gl	pl	sl
clown	**fl**ower	**gl**ue	**pl**ant	**sl**ide
br	cr	dr	fr	gr
bread	**cr**ayons	**dr**um	**fr**og	**gr**apes

Digraphs and Consonant Blends
Sound Chart (cont.)

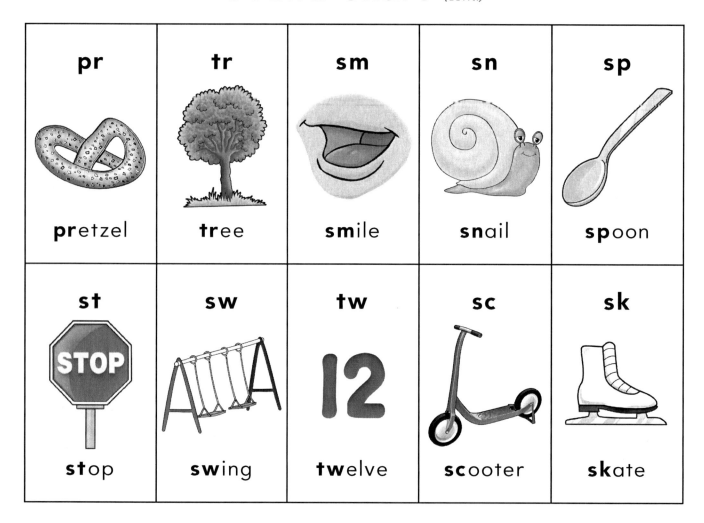

pr	tr	sm	sn	sp
pretzel	tree	smile	snail	spoon
st	sw	tw	sc	sk
stop	swing	twelve	scooter	skate

My Writing Checklist

Standard

Uses strategies to edit and publish written work

Materials

- *My Writing Checklist* (page 239; mywritingchecklist.pdf)
- Chart paper
- Marker

Mentor Texts

- *No, David!* by David Shannon
- See *Mentor Text List* in Appendix C for other suggestions.

Procedure

Note: Repeat this lesson until students develop automaticity with the writing checklist. You may wish to split the lesson into several days.

Think About Writing

1. Tell students that authors want to make sure the books they write do not have any errors so they can be easily read. They send their drafts to an editor to have it checked. As writers in school, we do not have that luxury. We need to learn to check our work carefully so it can be read easily.

2. Review a mentor text if desired, and emphasize that before this book was printed, the author wrote a draft that was then checked for accuracy by an editor.

Teach

3. Tell students, "Today I will show you how to check your writing for conventions to make sure it is correct."

4. Display *My Writing Checklist* (page 239) so students can see it. Briefly review each item that is on the checklist: name, capital letter, ending punctuation, spacing, correct spelling of high-frequency words, as well as making sure it makes sense.

5. Write a short story on a sheet of chart paper. Model how to go through each item on the checklist and examine your writing. You may wish to introduce one step per day until you have worked through the checklist.

Engage

6. Have students *Turn and Talk* to explain to partners how to use the checklist to check for conventions.

My Writing Checklist *(cont.)*

Apply

7. Remind students to check for conventions so they will be just like a real author and the reader will be able to understand their writing. Provide students with *My Writing Checklist* to put in their writing folders.

Write/Conference

8. Provide time for students to write. Students may require more support as you move into editing. Be ready to bring small groups together to reteach the editing lesson. You should have authentic literature available so that students may see how real books contain the appropriate conventions of writing.

Spotlight Strategy

9. Acknowledge students for using the editing checklist, by saying things like, "Great checking! Nicole is a true conventions checker!"

Share

10. Have students meet with partners to share how they edited their work. Remind partners to pay a compliment and ask a question to their partner. Provide approximately one minute for students to share.

Homework

Ask students to look around their houses for evidence of editing. Have students copy two sentences that include the capitals, ending punctuation, and words spelled correctly. Remind students that good writers are always good observers.

Name: _____ Date: _____

My Writing Checklist

☐ **Did I put my name on my paper?**

Juan

☐ **Did I start my sentences with a capital letter?**

My mom likes cats.

☐ **Did I end my sentences with punctuation?**

. ! ?

☐ **Did I use good spacing?**

The dog

☐ **Did I spell my words correctly?**

☐ **Did my story make sense when I read it?**

Perfect Punctuation

Standards

- Uses strategies to edit and publish written work
- Uses conventions of punctuation in written compositions

Materials

- *Perfect Punctuation Chart* (page 242; punctuationchart.pdf)
- 3" × 5" index cards
- Chart paper
- Markers

Mentor Texts

- *Knuffle Bunny* by Mo Willems
- *Knuffle Bunny Too* by Mo Willems
- See *Mentor Text List* in Appendix C for other suggestions.

Procedures

Note: Use mentor texts to preview and discuss punctuation over several days. Each day, emphasize a new punctuation mark. First grade students should practice periods, question marks, exclamation points, and commas. However, take the opportunity to identify other punctuation, such as quotation marks and parenthesis.

Think About Writing

1. Tell students that authors use resources to improve their writing and record their thinking in a way that looks right, sounds right, and makes sense.

2. Review a mentor text if desired, and emphasize the author's use of punctuation. For example, Mo Willems, the author of *Knuffle Bunny*, loaded his book with punctuation that helps to clarify his message. Ask students to imagine the chaos in reading *Knuffle Bunny* without the support of punctuation. Tell students that writing stories and books without any punctuation is like having a sandwich with no bread.

Teach

3. Tell students, "Over the next several days, I will show you how to check the punctuation in your writing." Explain that punctuation helps readers understand our stories.

4. Display the *Perfect Punctuation Chart* (page 242). Discuss each ending punctuation mark with students.

5. Write a period on an index card. Play "I Spy" with students to find periods in a mentor text. Repeat the procedure with a question mark and an exclamation point.

Perfect Punctuation *(cont.)*

6. Write the following sentences on chart paper without the ending punctuation.

   - We played in the snow(.)
     (**.**—telling me, declarative—use a period)

   - How did you build that snowman(?)
     (**?**—asking me, interrogative—use a question mark)

   - Wow, a snowman is really cool(!)
     (**!**—exciting, exclamatory—use an exclamation point)

   Discuss with students which ending punctuation should be placed at the end of each sentence. Write the correct ending punctuation.

Engage

7. Have students *Heads-up, Stand-up, Partner-up* and work with partners to name the different types of ending punctuation. Ask them to discuss how each ending punctuation makes sentences meaningful. Provide approximately two minutes for students to talk.

Apply

8. Distribute the *Perfect Punctuation Chart* to add to their writing folders. Remind students to use it as a tool as they are writing.

Write/Conference

9. Provide time for students to write. Stop by the desks of three or four students and confer with them only about conventions. As you look over their work, remember to have only one teaching point and be certain that you start your conference with a compliment.

Spotlight Strategy

10. Spotlight great punctuation. For example, "You are so smart to check over your sentences for ending punctuation. Natasha and her partner are becoming very familiar with each ending punctuation mark and are polishing up their work."

Share

11. Have students meet with partners to share what they wrote today. Provide a few minutes for students to talk. Then have two or three students sit in the Author's Chair to share their work. These students will serve as important role models for the other students.

Homework

Have students look through books to find sentences with each type of ending mark. Have students copy the sentences, including the ending punctuation. Have students be ready to share their ideas tomorrow.

Name: _____ Date: _____

Perfect Punctuation Chart

●	**period** stop sign for a telling sentence	I like to ride bikes. My bike is blue.
?	**question mark** stop sign for an asking sentence	Do you like bikes? Where is your bike?
!	**exclamation point** stop sign for an emotion sentence	Hooray! Let's go riding!

My Editing Guide

Standard

Uses strategies to edit and publish written work

Materials

- *Callie, Super Conventions Checker* (page 214; callie.pdf)
- *My Editing Guide* (page 245; myeditingguide.pdf)
- *Capital Rap* (page 220; capitalrap.pdf)
- Chart paper
- Markers

Mentor Texts

- *Alexander and the Terrible, Horrible, No Good, Very Bad Day* by Judith Viorst
- *If You Give a Mouse a Cookie* by Laura Numeroff
- See *Mentor Text List* in Appendix C for other suggestions.

Procedure

Note: You may wish to divide this lesson into three components: capitalization, punctuation, and spelling. Like many mini-lessons, this one can be revisited again and again. Make sure you have *Callie, Super Conventions Checker* (page 214) visible in the room. Refer to it often.

Think About Writing

1. Tell students that authors take charge of all phases of their learning. Explain that they will edit work from their writing folders.

2. Review a mentor text if desired, and emphasize the author's use of conventions to impact the message.

Teach

3. Tell students, "Today I will show you how to use the *My Editing Guide* (page 245) to fix your writing."

4. Review each item on the checklist with students. You may wish to create a large anchor chart to post in the classroom.

   - Capitalization—Remind students of the *Capital Rap* (page 220). Write the following sentence on chart paper and model editing it: *on thursday, I walked to lewisburg to see the movie, grown-ups.* Review with students how to use the editor's marks to show which words should be capitalized or made lowercase.

   - Punctuation—Remind students that punctuation moves the reader through the writing with excitement and understanding. Review with students the three ending punctuation marks and when they are used. Write some sample sentences on the chart paper. Distribute *My Editing Guide* to students and have them add missing ending marks, then place it in their writing folders.

My Editing Guide *(cont.)*

- Spelling—Review with students how to listen for the sounds in words and to use their eyes to determine if words look right. Write some sample sentences on the chart paper. Model using *My Editing Guide* to check the sentences. Demonstrate how to use editor's marks to indicate words that are misspelled.

Engage

5. Have students *Heads-up, Stand-up, Partner-up* and work with partners to practice editing a few sentences. Write the following sentences on chart paper: *dad took me to da store on saturday*

   Ask students to discuss capitalization, punctuation, and spelling. Encourage them to use *My Editing Guide* as they review the sentence.

Apply

6. Provide students with *My Editing Guide* to keep in their writing folders. Ask students to choose a piece from their writing folders to edit.

Write/Conference

7. Have students work with partners to edit the writing samples they chose. Remind students to use *My Editing Guide* for marks they can make to fix their writing. No conferencing today. Rotate around the room to provide praise, support, and guidance.

Spotlight Strategy

8. Spotlight great editing work. For example, "What clever writers! Christian is just focusing on periods."

Share

9. Have students meet with different partners to share how they improved their writing. Provide approximately two to three minutes.

Homework
Ask students to notice conversations they hear. Ask them to think about the punctuation that might be used to write what they have heard.

Name: _____ Date: _____

My Editing Guide

Editor's Marks	Meaning	Example
≡	**capitalize**	≡david gobbled up the grapes.
/	**make lowercase**	My mother hugged Me when I /came /Home.
(.) (?) (!)	**add ending punctuation**	The clouds danced in the sky (.)
(sp)	**spelling mistake**	sp I (laffed) at the story.

Essential Materials

Create a toolkit of items you can carry around with you as you conference with students. The toolkit can be a shoebox, a plastic tote, or anything you are comfortable carrying around from student to student. Any supplies that will help make your conference run smoothly are appropriate to put in the tote. Suggested items are listed below:

- Teacher Conferring Notebook
- Mentor text used for daily writing lesson (changes regularly)
- Highlighters or highlighting tape (to draw attention to words)
- Scissors, glue, tape, or a small stapler for revision, cutting, pasting, and moving around
- Sticky notes for making suggestions
- Colored pens for editing (green, red, blue, black)
  - Green—capitalization
  - Red—ending punctuation
  - Blue—spelling
  - Black—inserting
- Rubber band for stretching sentences
- Whiteboard or magnetic board with markers for modeling
- Magnetic chips or large colored buttons
- 1 package of correction tape or correction fluid
- Assorted paper

Conferring Notebook
Getting to the Core of Writing

Mini-Lesson Log

Date	Mini-Lesson Instructional Focus

Conference Log

P: Praise—What strategies did I notice the child using independently?

TP: Teaching Point—What teaching point will move this child forward in his or her development as a writer?

Name: Date: P: TP:	Name: Date: P: TP:	Name: Date: P: TP:	Name: Date: P: TP:
Name: Date: P: TP:	Name: Date: P: TP:	Name: Date: P: TP:	Name: Date: P: TP:
Name: Date: P: TP:	Name: Date: P: TP:	Name: Date: P: TP:	Name: Date: P: TP:

Conference Countdown

10 Conversation—The conversation should feel like a friendly chat with the student doing the most talking. Keep in mind, the person doing the most talking is doing the most learning.

9 It's about the WRITER, not the Writing—Teach the strategy that will support the writer after he or she is finished with this particular piece of writing. For example, do not just spell a word for a child, but teach him or her to segment the sounds to spell many words.

8 Focus on the Content—You are not there to simply fix up the conventions of a writing piece. When possible, have the student read the piece aloud before you even look at it and focus purely on the content. It's a challenge!

7 Observe, Praise, Guide, Connect—Establish a routine to become effective and efficient.

6 Begin with Praise!—Everyone likes a compliment. Beginning with a compliment gives students a sense of joy and pride in their work as well as recognizes developing writing skills.

5 Talk Like a Writer to a Writer—Use the language and vocabulary of a writer and respect the student's developmental level of writing.

4 Connect or not to Connect?—When conferring, only make connections to your daily mini-lesson when appropriate for the student's piece of writing.

3 Record and Reflect—Use your Conferring Notebook to monitor the progress of writing in your classroom and individual students. The information is valuable in defining your focus for writing instruction.

2 Variety—Incorporate a variety of activities that meet the multiple learning modalities of your students, like varying your conferring group sizes and using manipulatives.

1 Be There!—Your face and eyes tell it all. Let students know you truly care about the writing they are sharing with you.

Conferring Step-by-Step

The four phases of a conference structure are:

1. Observe
2. Praise
3. Guide
4. Connect

Observe—Use observation as a chance to build your background knowledge of the writer. During this element of the conference, you will determine what the writer knows and can do independently, and what the writer can do with support, called the zone of proximal development (Vygotsky 1978). Begin by asking yourself:

- What do I already know about this student's developmental level of writing and past writing from my conference notes and previous observations?

- What can I learn from the student's current writing piece and writing behaviors?

- What can I learn through questioning and listening to the writer?

When asking students about their writing work, open-ended questions provide guidance and support for students to begin reflecting on their writing. A close-ended question, such as, "Is this you in the picture?" elicits a simple one- or two-word response. An open-ended question, such as, "What can you tell me about your picture?" offers opportunities for the writer to explain and describe ideas, motives, and feelings about his or her work, ultimately gaining clarity and developing a deeper understanding of his or her writing. You might ask the writer:

- So, what are you working on in your writing today?

- What can you tell me about your important writing work?

Through your observation, you should determine a successful writing point and one teaching point that will help this child become a more independent writer. Selecting a teaching point can be daunting as we analyze a young writer's work. Teachers often ask, "How do you know what to work on when there are so many things?" The truth is there is no right answer. Here are some ideas to guide you as you select teaching points.

- Use what you know about the growth of this writer. Where is this writer developmentally?

- Consider what the student is working on at this time. What is the student's focus in his or her writing?

- Use the current writing curriculum and the Common Core State Standards.

- Use what is being taught in mini-lessons and whole-group instruction.

Where we ourselves are as writers, as well as where we are as teachers of writing, greatly affect our decisions. As you become more knowledgeable about the developmental phases of writers and the understanding of quality writing instruction, your decisions become more sophisticated. The more you confer with your writers, the more effective you become at making decisions during conferring. Most importantly, select one teaching point that will support each writer during your conference. Calkins (2003) reminds us to teach to the writer and not to the writing.

Conferring Step-by-Step *(cont.)*

Praise—Recognize the writer for work well done. Always begin a conference with a positive comment. This praise provides positive feedback intended to identify what the student is doing correctly and to encourage the writer to repeat that accomplishment in future writing. Isolate and identify the successful writing strategy in the student's writing piece. When praises are authentic and specific, they become a teachable moment. Below are some examples of powerful praise.

- "Something I really like that you've done is how you shared the setting with your reader. That's exactly what good writers do!"

- "I see here in your writing you chose to use color words to give your reader more details in your story. Wonderful words!"

- "Just like the authors we have been studying, you have an excellent picture that helps your reader visualize exactly what is happening in your story."

- "I am so impressed with the way you just got right to work and accomplished so much writing in such a short amount of time."

Guide—Personalize and scaffold instruction to meet the writer's needs. The instruction includes sharing the writing strategy you will teach the writer, demonstrating the strategy, and then guiding the writer through practicing the process. Teach the writer a personalized strategy based on your earlier decisions. When the decision is based on a previously taught mini-lesson, writers make additional connections and greater achievement is gained. As part of the routine of the mini-lesson, you must explicitly state what you will teach the student.

- Mentor texts and writing samples are excellent resources to weave into your conference instruction. Writers can visualize the craft you are teaching when they are exposed to concrete examples, particularly from real literature.

- Initial teaching remarks may include, "Let me show you something that good writers do…" and, "Sometimes in my writing, I try to…"

By offering support while the student practices the strategy, you increase the chances of success. Any time you engage students in the application of new strategies, you enhance the probability they will recall that strategy in future writing. Once the writer is engaged in practice, you may move on to confer with another writer. However, leave the writer with expectations until you return, such as, "When I get back, I want to see …" Upon your return, provide specific feedback relative to your expectations. For example, "Well done! Now I really have a picture in my mind of your character."

Conferring Step-by-Step (cont.)

Connect—Make connections between teaching and future writing. First, clearly restate what the writer learned and practiced. Then, remind and encourage the writer to use the strategy in future writing. As students become familiar with the conference structure, you may ask the student to share the new learning to get a sense of his or her understanding of your teaching. Making connections may begin as follows:

- "Remember, good writers always…"

- "Tell me what you just learned as a writer."

Writer's Workshop conferences will vary in length and type based on the time of year and the needs of your class. Conferences are most successful when routines and expectations have been established and young writers can manage their own writing time. At the beginning of the year, while establishing routines, drop-by conferences provide a quick glimpse into what each student is working on and what kind of help is needed. Once routines are established, meet with students in individual and/or small group conferences that are focused around specific needs. You may also include peer conferences, but this requires modeling, experience, and practice. For young writers, we use *Compliment and Question*. The compliment should be more than a general statement, such as, "I like your story." It should be specific to the writing, for example, "I like the way you ask a question to begin your story." A question should be something the peer would like to know more about or something that needs clarification.

The conference should be brief and reflect the child's age and development—usually not longer than 5–7 minutes in first grade. Small group conferences may be as long as 8–10 minutes as you will be checking in with each student. Hold the conference wherever you prefer. Some teachers prefer moving desk to desk or table to table while others prefer that students join them at a small conference table or on the floor. Remember these two points:

- *Have a seat!* Wherever you decide to hold your conferences, it is important that students know you are committed to giving them your attention. By sitting down, you are sending the message that you are there with them at that moment.

- *Be prepared!* Have materials readily available to you during the conference. You may wish to compile a Conferring Toolkit of essential materials (see page 246 of Appendix A) that can be carried with you or placed in your conference area.

Continuing to provide meaningful and relevant conferences requires some form of keeping notes during your writing conferences. A simple, but thorough conference summary can identify areas of writing deficiencies and strengths as you plan future mini-lessons, select students for small group conferences, and report student progress to parents. To support you as you make conferring a priority in Writer's Workshop, pages for the *Conferring Notebook* are included on pages 247–250.

Benchmark Assessment Overview

Administering a Benchmark (page 255) is a guide to assist you as you begin giving benchmarks. It is important that the prompt is uniform across classrooms when measuring growth at a school level. First grade benchmark prompts should be simple and attainable, for example:

- Draw a picture and write a story about your favorite food.

- Draw a picture and write a story about an animal. What does your animal look like? What does your animal eat? Where does it live? What is interesting about your animal?

- Write a story and tell about a special time you had with your mom (dad, grandma, grandpa, brother, friend). Be sure to include a beginning, middle, and end along with important details about your adventure.

The Writing Rubric (page 256; firstgradewritingrubric.pdf) is a tool to analyze student writing skills. You may refer to the Phases of Writing (pages 8–9) to further clarify your students' writing growth.

The Writing Report (page 257; firstgradewritingreport.pdf) serves as a summative report of a student's writing benchmarks. The completed form along with the beginning-, middle-, and end-of-year benchmarks are placed in the student's record folder at the end of the year.

The Grouping Mat (page 258 firstgradegroupingmat.pdf) is an at-a-glance chart showing which students in your classroom have attained particular benchmarks. Simply circle the current benchmark period, and complete the chart by recording your students' names in the boxes. Your goal is to see the students' names progressively move upward on the rubric report.

The core of writing instruction is the desire to support young writers as they explore, discover, and learn the writing process. It also involves determining what knowledge and skills young writers have developed over a period of time. Assessment is a continuous process and, when used properly, benefits teachers as well as students.

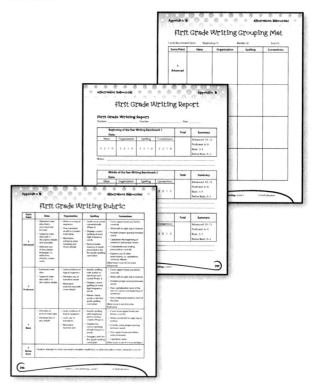

Administering a Benchmark

Writing Benchmarks are usually administered at the beginning, middle, and end of the school year to measure improvements and determine the writer's strengths and deficits in writing development. To get started, follow these guidelines:

- Administer the Writing Benchmark Prompt in small groups. This allows the teacher to observe and take anecdotal notes of individual student behaviors.

- It is important not to practice the prompt prior to the writing benchmark session.

- Do not provide teacher support. Your goal is to determine what students are able to do independently. If a student demonstrates frustration, he or she may just draw a picture, but you may wish to redirect the student to the prompt. Compliment the drawing and invite the student to write something about the drawing as best he or she can.

- Allow students to use classroom displays such as word walls. Note words copied from the word wall.

- Distribute paper to each student. Use paper familiar to the students. Students should write their name and the date on the back so that it is not seen prior to scoring the writing. This will help you to stay objective as you grade the writing piece .

- Supply pencils and crayons when necessary.

- Explain to your class that this process will show how much they have grown as writers and that a prompt will be given at the beginning, middle, and end of the year.

- Read the prompt to your students. Paraphrase the prompt when necessary to clarify understanding. You may wish to display the prompt on chart paper or on a whiteboard.

- Have each student read you his or her story upon completion. Keep a record of what each student wrote in your own writing so that you will be able to identify the words that he or she used. If some words are unreadable due to invented spelling, write them down at the bottom of the writing piece or on a sticky note.

First Grade Writing Rubric

Score Point	Ideas	Organization	Spelling	Conventions
3 Advanced	• Maintains main idea that is narrowed and focused • Supports main idea with 5+ descriptive details and examples • Attempts use of descriptive language, i.e., adjectives, adverbs, action verbs	• Writes in a logical sequence • Uses transition words to connect main ideas • Illustration enhances story meaning and shows details	• Spells many words conventionally (Phase 4) • Displays correct spelling of most high frequency words • Demonstrates mastery of words presented in the first grade spelling curriculum	• Forms upper/lowercase letters correctly • Writes left to right, top to bottom • Includes proper spacing between words • Capitalizes the beginning of sentences and proper nouns • Consistently uses ending punctuation correctly • Explores use of other punctuation, i.e., quotations, commas, ellipses (Must have 5 out of 6 to score Advanced)
2 Proficient	• Expresses main idea • Supports main idea with 3–4 descriptive details	• Some evidence of logical sequence • Attempts use of transition words • Illustration matches text with some details	• Invents spelling with a letter to represent each sound (Phase 3) • Displays correct spelling of some high frequency words • Masters many words in the first grade spelling curriculum	• Forms upper/lowercase letters correctly • Writes left to right, top to bottom • Includes proper spacing between words • Uses capitalization most of the time for names and beginning of sentences • Uses ending punctuation most of the time (Must score 4 out of 6 to be Proficient)
1 Basic	• Attempts to present main idea • Develops few, if any, details	• Lacks evidence of logical sequence • Lacks use of transitions • Illustration matches text	• Invents spelling with beginning and/or ending sounds (Phase 2) • Displays few correct spellings of high frequency words • Struggles with the first grade spelling curriculum	• Forms most upper/lowercase letters correctly • Writes mostly left to right, top to bottom • Includes some proper spacing between words • Uses upper/lowercase letters indiscriminately • Capitalizes name (Must score 3 out of 5 to score Basic)
0 Below Basic	• Student attempts to write, but result is illegible, insufficient, or otherwise fails to meet criteria for score of 1.			

First Grade Writing Report

First Grade Writing Report

Student: _____ Teacher: _____ Year: _____

Beginning of the Year Writing Benchmark 1 Date:				Total	Summary
Ideas	Organization	Spelling	Conventions		Advanced: 10–12
3 2 1 0	3 2 1 0	3 2 1 0	3 2 1 0		Proficient: 6–9 Basic: 3–5 Below Basic: 0–2

Notes: _____

_____

Middle of the Year Writing Benchmark 2 Date:				Total	Summary
Ideas	Organization	Spelling	Conventions		Advanced: 10–12
3 2 1 0	3 2 1 0	3 2 1 0	3 2 1 0		Proficient: 6–9 Basic: 3–5 Below Basic: 0–2

Notes: _____

_____

End of the Year Writing Benchmark 3 Date:				Total	Summary
Ideas	Organization	Spelling	Conventions		Advanced: 10–12
3 2 1 0	3 2 1 0	3 2 1 0	3 2 1 0		Proficient: 6–9 Basic: 3–5 Below Basic: 0–2

Notes: _____

_____

First Grade Writing Grouping Mat

Circle Benchmark Term: Beginning (1)   Middle (2)   End (3)

Score Point	Ideas	Organization	Spelling	Conventions
3 **Advanced**				
2 **Proficient**				
1 **Basic**				
0 **Below** **Basic**				

Benchmark Writing Samples

Beginning of the Year

Prompt: Draw and write about yourself and something you like to do.

Text: My name is Jackson. I like pizza. My phone number is 304-222-XXXX.

Beginning of the Year Writing Benchmark 1 Date:				Total	Summary
Ideas	Organization	Spelling	Conventions		Advanced: 10–12
3 2 (1) 0	3 2 (1) 0	3 2 (1) 0	3 2 (1) 0	4 Basic	Proficient: 6–9 Basic: 3–5 Below Basic: 0–2

Notes:

PESE for *pizza* = Phase 2

FON for *phone* = Phase 3

Benchmark Writing Samples *(cont.)*

Middle of the Year

Prompt: We have been learning about many different kinds of animals. Draw and write a story about an animal.

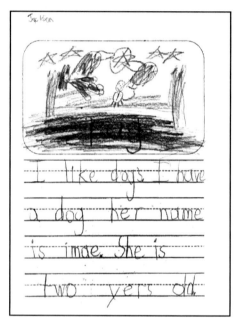
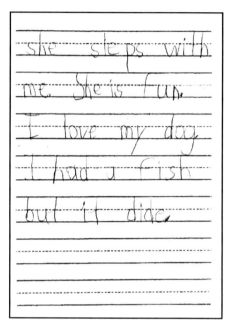

Text: I like dogs. I have a dog. Her name is Imae. She is two years old. She sleeps with me. She is fun. I love my dog. I had a fish but it died.

Middle of the Year Writing Benchmark 2 Date:				Total	Summary
Ideas	Organization	Spelling	Conventions	8 Proficient	Advanced: 10–12 Proficient: 6–9 Basic: 3–5 Below Basic: 0–2
3 (2) 1 0	3 (2) 1 0	3 (2) 1 0	3 (2) 1 0		

Notes:

YERS for *years* = Phase 3

SLEPS for *sleeps* = Phase 3

DIDE for *died* = Phase 4

Benchmark Writing Samples (cont.)

End of the Year

Prompt: Draw and write about what you enjoy doing in your free time.

Text: When it is my free time I swim. I swim in the deep end. I swim fast. I hope to win a trophy.
I hope I will be the best. After swimming I will go home and take a nap. What do you like to do?
I beat my dad and my sister. I beat my cousins too. I also beat my friends. I swim at Steely Pool.
My coach is Christi Fubio. She is very nice.

End of the Year Writing Benchmark 3 Date:				Total	Summary
Ideas	Organization	Spelling	Conventions		Advanced: 10–12
(3) 2 1 0	(3) 2 1 0	(3) 2 1 0	(3) 2 1 0	12 Advanced	Proficient: 6–9 Basic: 3–5 Below Basic: 0–2

Notes:

HOP for *hope* = Phase 3

TROFY for *trophy* = Phase 4

SWIMING for *swimming* = Phase 4

COUZEN for *cousin* = Phase 4

ALLSOW for *also* = Phase 4

COUCH for *coach* = Phase 4

Mentor Text List

The books listed below exemplify the trait under which they are listed. Many of the titles are listed as mentor texts in specific lessons and others are listed as a resource for you to use for read alouds and discussion.

Managing Writer's Workshop

Binkow, Howard. 2006. *Howard B. Wigglebottom Learns to Listen*. Minneapolis, MN: Lerner Publishing Group.

Cook, Julia. 2006. *My Mouth is a Volcano!* Chattanooga, TN: National Center for Youth Issues.

———. 2007. *Personal Space Camp*. Chattanooga, TN: National Center for Youth Issues.

———. 2011. *The Worst Day of My Life Ever!* Boys Town, NE: Boys Town Press.

Curtis, Jamie Lee. 2004. *It's Hard to Be Five: Learning How to Work My Control Panel*. New York: HarperCollins.

Lester, Helen. 1995. *Me First*. Boston: Sandpiper.

———. 1997. *Listen, Buddy!* Boston: Sandpiper.

———. 2012. *All for Me and None for All*. Boston: Houghton Mifflin Books for Children.

Lionni, Leo. 1973. *Swimmy*. New York: Dragonfly Books.

McGovern, Ann. 1992. *Too Much Noise*. Boston: Sandpiper.

Munsch, Robert. 2002. *We Share Everything*. New York: Cartwheel Books.

Reiss, Mike. 2008. *The Boy Who Wouldn't Share*. New York: HarperCollins.

Shannon, David. 1998. *No, David!* New York: Blue Sky Press.

———. 1999. *David Goes to School*. New York: Blue Sky Press.

Print Concepts

Bayer, Jane E. 1992. *A, My Name Is Alice*. New York: Puffin.

Carlson, Nancy. 1999. *ABC I Like Me!* New York: Puffin.

Ehlert, Lois. 1994. *Eating the Alphabet: Fruits & Vegetables from A to Z*. Boston: Sandpiper.

Fleming, Denise. 2002. *Alphabet Under Construction*. New York: Henry Holt and Co.

Johnson, Stephen. 1999. *Alphabet City*. New York: Puffin.

Lionni, Leo. 1990. *The Alphabet Tree*. New York: Dragonfly Books.

Martin Jr., Bill, and John Archambault. 2009. *Chicka Chicka Boom Boom*. New York: Simon & Schuster Books for Young Readers.

Pallotta, Jerry. 1992. *The Vegetable Alphabet Book*. Watertown, MA: Charlesbridge Publishing.

Wood, Audrey. 2001. *Alphabet Adventure*. New York: Blue Sky Press.

Mentor Text List (cont.)

Ideas

Aliki. 1987. *We Are Best Friends*. New York: Greenwillow Books.

———. 1991. *My Five Senses*. New York: Harper Festival.

Appelt, Kathi. 2003. *Incredible Me!* New York: HarperCollins.

Asch, Frank. 1984. *Just Like Daddy*. New York: Aladdin.

Bayer, Jane E. 1992. *A, My Name Is Alice*. New York: Puffin.

Beaumont, Karen. 2004. *I Like Myself!* Boston: Harcourt Children's Books.

Bottner, Barbara, and Gerald Kruglik. 2004. *Wallace's Lists*. New York: Katherine Tegen Books.

Boyd, Candy Dawson. 1998. *Daddy, Daddy, Be There*. New York: Puffin.

Browne, Anthony. 2009. *My Mom*. New York: Farrar, Straus and Giroux.

Bulla, Clyde Robert. 2001. *A Tree is a Plant*. New York: Collins.

Carlson, Nancy. 1999. *ABC I Like Me!* New York: Puffin.

Caseley, Judith. 1994. *Dear Annie*. New York: Greenwillow Books.

Cooper, Sharon Katz. 2006. *Whose Hat Is This?: A Look at Hats Workers Wear–Hard, Tall, and Shiny*. Mankato, MN: Picture Window Books.

Curtis, Jamie Lee. 2002. *I'm Gonna Like Me: Letting Off a Little Self-Esteem*. New York: HarperCollins.

———. 2004. *It's Hard to Be Five: Learning How to Work My Control Panel*. New York: HarperCollins.

Galdone, Paul. 2006. *Little Red Hen*. Boston: Sandpiper.

Gibbons, Gail. 1994. *Frogs*. New York: Holiday House.

———. 2000. *Bats*. New York: Holiday House.

———. 2004. *The Pumpkin Book*. Pine Plains, NY: Live Oak Media.

———. 2011. *Apples*. Pine Plains, NY: Live Oak Media.

Hallinan, P. K. 2002. *When I Grow Up*. Nashville: Ideals Publications.

Henkes, Kevin. 1991. *Chrysanthemum*. New York: Greenwillow Books.

Kellogg, Steven. 1990. *Best Friends*. New York: Puffin.

LeSieg, Theo. 1993. *I Can Write! A Book By Me, Myself.* New York: Random House Books for Young Readers.

Liebman, Dan. 2000. *I Want to Be a Doctor*. Ontario: Firefly Books Ltd.

Lionni, Leo. 1973. *Swimmy*. New York: Dragonfly Books.

Litwin, Eric. 2011. *Pete the Cat: Rocking In My School Shoes*. New York: HarperCollins.

MacLachlan, Patricia. 1994. *All the Places to Love*. New York: HarperCollins.

Mentor Text List (cont.)

Ideas (cont.)

Mayer, Mercer. 2001. *Just Me and My Dad*. New York: Random House Books for Young Readers.

———. 2001. *Just Me and My Mom*. New York: Random House Books for Young Readers.

———. 2001. *Just My Friend and Me*. New York: Random House Books for Young Readers.

Miller, Margaret. 1998. *My Five Senses*. New York: Aladdin.

Munsch, Robert. 1995. *Love You Forever*. Ontario: Firefly Books Ltd.

Penn, Audrey. 2007. *The Kissing Hand*. Terre Haute, IN: Tanglewood Press.

Pfeffer, Wendy. 2004. *From Seed to Pumpkin*. New York: Collins.

Rylant, Cynthia. 2004. *The Relatives Came*. New York: Atheneum Books for Young Readers.

Viorst, Judith. 2009. *Alexander and the Terrible, Horrible, No Good, Very Bad Day*. New York: Atheneum Books for Young Readers.

Willems, Mo. 2004. *Knuffle Bunny: A Cautionary Tale*. New York: Hyperion.

———. 2007. *Knuffle Bunny Too: A Case of Mistaken Identity*. New York: Hyperion.

Williams, Vera B. 1984. *A Chair for My Mother*. New York: Greenwillow Books.

Sentence Fluency

Aylesworth, Jim. 1995. *Old Black Fly*. New York: Henry Holt and Co.

Beaumont, Karen. 2005. *I Ain't Gonna Paint No More!* Boston: Harcourt Children's Books.

Brown, Margaret Wise. 1990. *The Important Book*. New York: HarperCollins.

———. 2005. *The Runaway Bunny*. New York: HarperCollins.

Carle, Eric. 1994. *The Very Hungry Caterpillar*. New York: Philomel Books.

Charlip, Remy. 1993. *Fortunately*. New York: Aladdin.

Henkes, Kevin. 1991. *Chrysanthemum*. New York: Greenwillow Books.

Hoban, Tana. 2008. *Over, Under and Through*. New York: Aladdin.

Hutchins, Pat. 1971. *Rosie's Walk*. New York: Aladdin.

Kalan, Robert. 2004. *Jump, Frog, Jump*. Pine Plains, NY: Live Oak Media.

Martin Jr., Bill. 1997. *Polar Bear, Polar Bear, What Do You Hear?* New York: Henry Holt and Co.

———. 1992. *Brown Bear, Brown Bear, What Do You See?* New York: Henry Holt and Co.

Palatini, Margie. 2003. *Bedhead*. New York: Simon & Schuster Books for Young Readers.

Randell, Beverley, Jenny Giles, and Annette Smith. 1996. *Moms and Dads*. Boston: Rigby.

Mentor Text List (cont.)

Sentence Fluency (cont.)

Rosen, Michael. 1997. *We're Going On a Bear Hunt*. New York: Little Simon.

Rylant, Cynthia. 2004. *The Relatives Came*. New York: Atheneum Books for Young Readers.

Smucker, Anna. 1994. *No Star Nights*. New York: Dragonfly Books.

———. 1995. *Outside the Window*. New York: Random House Value Publishing.

Williams, Sue. 2004. *I Went Walking*. Pine Plains, NY: Live Oak Media.

Williams, Vera B. 1984. *A Chair for My Mother*. New York: Greenwillow Books.

Organization

Ada, Alma Flor. 2001. *Yours Truly, Goldilocks*. New York: Atheneum Books for Young Readers.

———. 2004. *With Love, Little Red Hen*. New York: Atheneum Books for Young Readers.

Ahlberg, Allan. 2001. *The Jolly Postman*. New York: LB Kids.

Aliki. 1991. *My Five Senses*. New York: HarperFestival.

Arnosky, Jim. 2008. *All About Frogs*. New York: Scholastic Inc.

Asch, Frank. 2008. *The Sun Is My Favorite Star*. Boston: Sandpiper.

Bayer, Jane E. 1992. *A, My Name Is Alice*. New York: Puffin.

Brett, Jan. 1996. *Goldilocks and the Three Bears*. New York: Puffin.

Buehner, Caralyn. 2010. *The Escape of Marvin the Ape*. Logan, IA: Perfection Learning.

Bunting, Eve. 1989. *The Wednesday Surprise*. New York: Clarion Books.

Carle, Eric. 1996. *The Grouchy Ladybug*. New York: HarperCollins.

———. 2009. *The Tiny Seed*. New York: Little Simon.

Carlson, Nancy. 1999. *ABC I Like Me!* New York: Puffin.

Caseley, Judith. 1994. *Dear Annie*. New York: Greenwillow Books.

Cole, Joanna. 2001. *Magic School Bus Explores the Senses*. New York: Scholastic.

Cooper, Sharon Katz. 2006. *Whose Hat Is This?: A Look at Hats Workers Wear–Hard, Tall, and Shiny*. Mankato, MN: Picture Window Books.

Cowley, Joy. 1998. *Wishy-Washy Day*. Columbus, OH: Wright Group.

———. 2006. *Mrs. Wishy-Washy's Farm*. New York: Puffin.

Cronin, Doreen. 2011. *Click, Clack, Moo: Cows That Type*. New York: Little Simon.

dePaola, Tomie. 1978. *Pancakes for Breakfast*. Boston: Sandpiper.

Feelings, Muriel. 1992. *Jambo Means Hello: Swahili Alphabet*. New York: Puffin.

Mentor Text List (cont.)

Organization (cont.)

Gibbons, Gail. 2005. *Chicks and Chickens*. New York: Holiday House.

Harrison, Joanna. 1995. *Dear Bear*. Minneapolis, MN: Carolrhoda Books.

Henkes, Kevin. 1991. *Chrysanthemum*. New York: Greenwillow Books.

Hummon, David. 1999. *Animal Acrostics*. Nevada City, CA: Dawn Publications.

James, Simon. 1996. *Dear Mr. Blueberry*. New York: Aladdin.

Keats, Ezra Jack. 1976. *The Snowy Day*. New York Puffin.

———. 1998. *A Letter to Amy*. New York: Puffin.

———. 1998. *Peter's Chair*. New York: Puffin.

Kitchen, Bert. 1992. *Animal Alphabet*. New York: Puffin.

Krauss, Ruth. 2004. *The Carrot Seed*. New York: HarperCollins.

Leedy, Loreen. 2005. *Look at My Book: How Kids Can Write & Illustrate Terrific Books*. New York: Holiday House.

Lollis, Sylvia, and Joyce Hogan. 2002. *Should We Have Pets?: A Persuasive Text*. New York: Mondo Publishing.

MacDonald, Wendy. 2000. *Training a Guide Dog*. Boston: Rigby.

Mayer, Mercer. 2001. *All By Myself*. New York: Random House Books for Young Readers.

Miller, Jane. 1987. *Farm Alphabet Book*. New York: Scholastic Paperback.

Numeroff, Laura. 1985. *If You Give a Mouse a Cookie*. New York: HarperCollins.

Orloff, Karen Kaufman. 2004. *I Wanna Iguana*. New York: Putnam.

———. 2010. *I Wanna New Room*. New York: Putnam Juvenile.

Prelutsky, Jack. 1986. *Read Aloud Rhymes for the Very Young*. New York: Knopf Books for Young Reader.

Robbins, Ken. 2005. *Seeds*. New York: Atheneum Books for Young Readers.

Rylant, Cynthia. 2004. *The Relatives Came*. New York: Atheneum Books for Young Readers.

Schnur, Steven. 1997. *Autumn: An Alphabet Acrostic*. New York: Clarion Books.

———. 1999. *Spring: An Alphabet Acrostic*. New York: Clarion Books

———. 2001. *Summer: An Alphabet Acrostic*. New York: Clarion Books.

———. 2002. *Winter: An Alphabet Acrostic*. New York: Clarion Books.

Sendak, Maurice. 1988. *Where the Wild Things Are*. New York: HarperCollins.

Silverstein, Shel. 2004. *Where the Sidewalk Ends*. New York: HarperCollins.

Tuckfield, Liyala. 2000. *How to Make a Bird Feeder*. Boston: Rigby.

Mentor Text List (cont.)

Organization (cont.)

Viorst, Judith. 2009. *Alexander and the Terrible, Horrible, No Good, Very Bad Day*. New York: Atheneum Books for Young Readers.

Westcott, Nadine B. 1992. *Peanut Butter and Jelly: A Play Rhyme*. New York: Puffin.

Willems, Mo. 2003. *Don't Let the Pigeon Drive the Bus!* New York: Hyperion Press.

———. 2007. *Knuffle Bunny Too: A Case of Mistaken Identity*. New York: Hyperion.

Wood, Audrey. 2001. *Alphabet Adventure*. New York: Blue Sky Press.

———. 2004. *Alphabet Mystery*. New York: Scholastic.

Yolen, Jane, and Andrew Peters. 2007. *Here's a Little Poem: A Very First Book of Poetry*. Somerville, MA: Candlewick.

Word Choice

Aliki. 1986. *Feelings*. New York: Greenwillow Books.

———. 1991. *My Five Senses*. New York: HarperFestival.

Arnosky, Jim. 2000. *Rattlesnake Dance*. New York: Putnam Juvenile

Bang, Molly. 2004. *When Sophie Gets Angry–Really, Really Angry....* New York: Scholastic Paperbacks.

Banks, Kate. 2006. *Max's Words*. New York: Farrar, Straus and Giroux.

Boswell, Addie. 2008. *The Rain Stomper*. Tarrytown, NY: Marshall Cavendish Children's Books.

Buzzeo, Toni. 2004. *Little Loon and Papa*. New York: Dial.

Carlson, Nancy. 1999. *ABC I Like Me!* New York: Puffin.

Cherry, Lynne. 2003. *How Groundhog's Garden Grew*. New York: Blue Sky Press.

Coffelt, Nancy. 2009. *Big, Bigger, Biggest!* New York: Henry Holt and Co.

Cronin, Doreen. 2002. *Giggle, Giggle, Quack*. New York: Atheneum Books for Young Readers.

———. 2011. *Click, Clack, Moo: Cows That Type*. New York: Little Simon.

Crummel, Susan S., and Janet Stevens. 2005. *The Great Fuzz Frenzy*. Boston: Harcourt Children's Books.

Curtis, Jamie Lee. 1998. *Today I Feel Silly: & Other Moods That Make My Day*. New York: HarperCollins.

Davies, Nicola. 2004. *Bat Loves the Night*. Somerville, MA: Candlewick.

Falwell, Cathryn. 2006. *Word Wizard*. Boston: Sandpiper.

Faulkner, Kevin. 1999. *The Big Yawn*. Minneapolis, MN: Millbrook Press.

Fox, Mem. 1994. *Tough Boris*. Boston: Harcourt Children's Books.

Hall, Donald. 1994. *I Am the Dog I Am the Cat*. New York: Dial Books for Young Readers.

Haseley, Dennis. 2002. *A Story for Bear*. Boston: Harcourt Children's Books.

Mentor Text List *(cont.)*

Word Choice *(cont.)*

Henkes, Kevin. 2005. *Lilly's Purple Plastic Purse*. Pine Plains, NY: Live Oak Media.

———. 1991. *Chrysanthemum*. New York: Greenwillow Books.

Hillman, Ben. 2007. *How Big Is It?* New York: Scholastic Reference.

Hoose, Phillip M., Hannah Hoose, and Debbie Tilley. 1998. *Hey, Little Ant*. New York: Tricycle Press.

Jenkins, Steve. 1996. *Big and Little*. Boston: Houghton Mifflin Books for Children.

Jonas, Ann. 1989. *Color Dance*. New York: Greenwillow Books.

Kachenmeister, Cherryl. 2001. *On Monday When It Rained*. Boston: Sandpiper.

Kasza, Keiko. 2005. *My Lucky Day*. New York: Puffin.

Keats, Ezra Jack. 1976. *The Snowy Day*. New York Puffin.

———. 2001. *Pet Show!* New York: Puffin.

Kirk, Daniel. 2003. *Dogs Rule!* New York: Hyperion.

Lionni, Leo. 2006. *A Color of His Own*. New York: Knopf Books for Young Readers.

Litwin, Eric. 2010. *Pete the Cat: I Love My White Shoes*. New York: HarperCollins.

Long, Melina. 2003. *How I Became a Pirate*. Boston: Harcourt, Inc.

MacDonald, Ross. 2003. *Achoo! Bang! Crash! The Noisy Alphabet*. New York: Roaring Book Press.

MacLachlan, Patricia. 1998. *What You Know First*. New York: HarperCollins.

Miranda, Anne, and Ed Emberley. 1997. *Glad Monster, Sad Monster*. New York: LB Kids.

Munsch, Robert. 1985. *Mortimer*. Buffalo, NY: Annick Press.

———. 2002. *Andrew's Loose Tooth*. New York: Cartwheel.

O'Connor, Jane. 2008. *Fancy Nancy's Favorite Fancy Words: From Accessory to Zany*. New York: HarperCollins.

O'Malley, Kevin. 2005. *Once Upon a Cool Motorcycle Dude*. New York: Walker Children's.

Orloff, Karen Kaufman. 2004. *I Wanna Iguana*. New York: Putnam.

Palatini, Margie. 2000. *Zoom Broom*. New York: Hyperion Paperbacks for Children.

Ryan, Pam Muñoz. 2001. *Hello Ocean*. Watertown, MA: Talewinds.

Rylant, Cynthia. 1991. *Night in the Country*. New York: Atheneum Books for Young Readers.

Steinberg, Laya. 2005. *Thesaurus Rex*. Cambridge, MA: Barefoot Books.

Walton, Rick. 2001. *That's My Dog*. New York: Putnam Juvenile.

Williams, Linda D. 1988. *The Little Old Lady Who Was Not Afraid of Anything*. New York: HarperCollins.

Wilson, Karma. 2002. *Bear Snores On*. New York: Margaret McElderry Books.

Wood, Don, and Audrey Wood. 1989. *The Little Mouse, The Red Ripe Strawberry, and the Big Hungry Bear*. Swindon, England: Child's Play International

Mentor Text List (cont.)

Voice

Hall, Donald. 1994. *I Am the Dog I Am the Cat*. New York. Dial Books for Young Readers.

Henkes, Kevin. 1991. *Chrysanthemum*. New York. Greenwillow Books.

Kachenmeister, Cherryl. 1989. *On Monday, When It Rained. Boston*. Houghton Mifflin.

Shannon, David. 1998. *No, David!* New York. Blue Sky Press.

Williams, Linda D. 1988. *The Little Old Lady Who Was Not Afraid of Anything*. New York: HarperCollins.

Williams, Sue. 2004. *I Went Walking*. Pine Plains, NY: Live Oak Media.

Wilson, Karma. 2002. *Bear Snores*. New York. Margaret K. McElderry Books.

Conventions

Bayer, Jane E. 1992. *A, My Name Is Alice*. New York: Puffin.

Beaumont, Karen. 2004. *I Like Myself!* Boston: Harcourt Children's Books.

Cleary, Brian. 2008. *The Frail Snail on the Trail*. Minneapolis, MN: Millbrook Press.

Crummel, Susan S., and J. Stevens. 2005. *The Great Fuzz Frenzy*. Boston: Harcourt Children's Books.

Dr. Seuss. 1957. *The Cat in the Hat*. New York: Random House Books for Young Readers.

Eastman, Phillip D. 1960. *Are You My Mother?* New York: Random House Books for Young Reader.

Galdone, Paul. 2011. *Little Red Hen*. Boston: Sandpiper.

Hall, Pamela. 2009. *Punk-tuation Celebration*. Minneapolis, MN: Magic Wagon

Kachenmeister, Cherryl. 1989. *On Monday When It Rained*. Boston, Sandpiper.

Karling, Nurit. 1998. *The Fat Cat Sat on the Mat*. New York: HarperCollins .

Keats, Ezra Jack. 1996. *Whistle for Willie*. Pine Plains, NY: Live Oak Media.

Numeroff, Laura. 1985. *If You Give a Mouse a Cookie*. New York: HarperCollins.

Shannon, David. 1998. *No, David!* New York: Blue Sky Press.

Shaw, Nancy. 1986. *Sheep in a Jeep*. Boston: Houghton Mifflin Harcourt.

Shulevitz, Uri. 2003. *One Monday Morning*. New York: Farrar, Straus and Giroux.

Viorst, Judith. 2009. *Alexander and the Terrible, Horrible, No Good, Very Bad Day*. New York: Atheneum Books for Young Readers.

Ward, Cindy. 1997. *Cookie's Week*. New York: Puffin.

Willems, Mo. 2004. *Knuffle Bunny: A Cautionary Tale*. New York: Hyperion.

———. 2007. *Knuffle Bunny Too: A Case of Mistaken Identity*. New York: Hyperion.

Williams, Vera B. 1984. *A Chair for My Mother*. New York: Greenwillow Books.

Wood, Audrey. 2004. *Alphabet Mystery*. New York: Scholastic.

Writing Topics

There are many different topics that students can write about during Writer's Workshop. The chart below depicts the types of topics that students may be interested in, divided by months.

August/September	October	November	December	January
summer fun	animal habitats	Election Day	five senses	New Year's Day
apples	Christopher Columbus	Family	gingerbread	100th Day
community	exercise	farm animals	holiday	cooperation
fall	fire prevention	habitats and needs	winter	fables
family	foods we eat	harvest	visiting relatives	helping others
favorites	germs	leaves		manners
friends	Halloween	The Mayflower		Martin Luther King Jr.
Grandparent's Day	healthy habits	Pilgrims		penguins
me	pumpkins	Pocahontas		safety
pets	spiders	Thanksgiving		electricity
school		Veteran's Day		snow/snow day

February	March	April	May	June
dental health	American heroes	art	gardens	Father's Day
feelings	spring	chicks	Mother's Day	ocean/sea life
friends/friendship	Dr. Seuss	Earth Day	plants and trees	other countries
groundhogs	frogs	flowers	life cycles	vacations
pen pals	space and solar system	poetry	our environment	
presidents	Saint Patrick's Day	weather		
Valentine's Day	weather			
	storms, wind, rain			

Ideas from Literature

The mini-lesson, *Getting Ideas from Literature* (page 70), can be adapted and used with numerous texts. Listed below are only a few favorites. Although this list contains only books, keep in mind that ideas can be found in other media as well, such as pictures, magazines, newspapers, videos, Internet exploration, and books online, as well as many other places.

Texts	Idea Topics
Best Friends by Steven Kellogg *Just My Friend and Me* by Mercer Mayer *We Are Best Friends* by Steven Kellogg	Draw or write about your best friend Write a "how-to" be a good friend book
Knuffle Bunny by Mo Willems	A time you lost something An errand you do with Mommy/Daddy
The Pumpkin Book by Gail Gibbons	How do pumpkins grow? How to grow pumpkins Recipe for pumpkin pie/soup/bread
The Relatives Came by Cynthia Rylant	Visits to a relative's home A special vacation A favorite relative
The Snowy Day by Ezra Jack Keats	What do you like to do on a snowy day? How-to get ready to go outside How-to build a snowman How-to make hot chocolate
Cookie's Week by Cindy Ward *On Mondays When It Rained* by Cheryl Kachenmeister	Draw/Write a Days of the Week book Draw/Write a Months of the Year book
I Wanna Iguana by Karen Kaufman Orloff *I Wanna New Room* by Karen Kaufman Orloff	Write about something you want and why Write a letter
Bats by Gail Gibbons *Frogs* by Gail Gibbons	Write facts about an animal or insect of your choice
Just Me and My Mom by Mercer Mayer *Just Me and My Dad* by Mercer Mayer *Just Me and Grandma* by Mercer Mayer	Write about a special day with your mom, dad, grandma, etc.
Alexander and the Terrible, Horrible, No Good, Very Bad Day by Judith Viorst	Write about your worst day ever Write about your best day ever
Peter's Chair by Ezra Jack Keats *It's Hard to Be Five* by Jamie Lee Curtis	Write about things you can do now that you could not do when you were younger
I Like Myself! by Karen Beaumont *I Like Me!* by Nancy Carlson *I'm Gonna Like Me* by Jamie Lee Curtis	Write an "All About Me" or "I am Special!" book Write an "All About My Friend" book

Name: _____ Date: _____

Writing Paper 1

Name: _____ **Date:** _____

Writing Paper 2

Name: _____ Date: _____

Writing Paper 3

🙂

Supporting with Technology

Whether communicating via cell phones, texts, blogs, tweets, Facebook, email or gathering information via Internet, Google, and eBooks, today's students will live in a world increasingly shaped by technology. For this reason, Common Core State Standards highlight the effective use of technology-integrated instruction across the curriculum. Incorporating technology into instruction increases opportunities for students to be active learners, rather than passive receivers of information, and offers new ways of learning and sharing information.

The challenge for most teachers is how to seamlessly integrate technology use so that it does not take time away from writing instruction but enhances that instruction and increases students' interest and involvement. While uses of technology are seemingly limitless and constantly being updated, here are seven important ways teachers are successfully integrating technology into Writer's Workshop:

1. Digital and flip cameras can add excitement to any writing project. Student projects that capture pictures of the life cycle of a chick or a class field trip instantly invite students into a writing project. Digital photos can be used to generate a photo album of writing ideas, organize storyboards, promote language and vocabulary, illustrate student writing, and even be included in slide show presentations.

2. Document cameras are easily integrated in writing lessons and activities by both teachers and students. The benefits of using mentor texts for modeling are sometimes lost on students who may not be close enough to see the specific texts. Whether presenting photographs to gather writing ideas, sharing multiple beginnings from mentor texts, or displaying leaves and fossils to model descriptive language, the document camera offers a myriad of opportunities for modeling writing instruction for all students to see. Using the document camera allows you to zoom in on specific text features and details in illustrations. Students frequently volunteer to display their writing with the document camera and gather feedback from classmates on revising and editing. Teachers and students also enjoy presenting examples of good writing work and highlighting quality features in writing using the document camera.

3. Interactive whiteboards can serve a number of purposes for writing instruction. They provide the opportunity for student engagement and involvement of almost any materials or activity that can be viewed on a computer screen. Consider using the interactive whiteboard to teach whole group keyboarding skills, revising word choice by highlighting verbs or adjectives, using editing marks, building story webs, or reinforcing skills by accessing interactive websites. Of course, whiteboards are an excellent source to demonstrate and model lessons, present presentations and create class books and word banks.

Supporting with Technology *(cont.)*

4. Publishing tools abound in the technology realm. Students may be involved in illustrating their writing with Microsoft® Paint or a software program like KidPix®. Through word processing, students can create letters, essays, brochures, and even class newsletters. Many teachers use Microsoft® PowerPoint for publishing individual, team, or class writing projects, which can easily be printed and bound into classroom books or saved as eBooks. Podcasts are used to record students as they read their writing. This can support the revising and editing process as they listen carefully to their writing and add a special touch to a final published project. Technology enhances the writer's options for publishing their work. For example, parents and students enjoy viewing and listening to final projects on the school website.

5. Research has never been easier. Though writing teachers must be cognizant of Internet safety, misuse, plagiarism, and follow district policies, they know technology allows for new and purposeful ways to gather and synthesize research. Writing teachers demonstrate technology-driven research procedures and help students locate and bookmark trusted websites. Collaborating with colleagues about their student research websites can make research easy and accessible.

6. URLs (Uniform Resource Locator) are great to include in your classroom newsletter. Offer links for students to practice skills, view presentations, or learn about future topics like Arbor Day. And don't forget the authors! With activities like Ralph Fletcher's *Tips for Young Writers*, Patricia Pollacco's *Who Am I*, or *Poetry Writing with Jack Prelutsky*, author websites are filled with an assortment of information and activities to engage and motivate student writing. Visit author sites while teaching students how to create their own Author's Page. The possibilities are limitless.

7. Collaborative writing projects like ePals and virtual field trips open classroom boundaries to endless learning opportunities. EPals is a modern pen pal project in which students can collaborate on academic and cultural projects as well as establish everlasting friendships in other districts, states, or countries. Virtual field trips (VFT) offer learning opportunities that might otherwise be limited by distance and funding. Writing projects may be further enhanced by a virtual visit to the San Diego Zoo to learn about animal characteristics and habitats or to the National Aeronautics and Space Administration (NASA) to interview an astronaut.

Terminology Used

In order to adequately implement the lessons included in *Getting to the Core of Writing*, it is necessary to understand the terminology used throughout the resources.

Analytics—In order to be consistent with National Assessment of Educational Progress (NAEP) standards, the following analytics are used when describing writing proficiency:

- **Below Basic/Score 0**—Writing demonstrates an attempt to write, but the result is illegible, insufficient, or otherwise fails to meet the criteria for a score of 1.

- **Basic/Score 1**—Writing demonstrates little or marginal skill in responding to the writing benchmark tasks. Few traits of quality writing are present.

- **Proficient/Score 2**—Writing demonstrates developing skills in responding to the writing benchmark tasks. Most traits of quality writing are evident.

- **Advanced/Score 3**—Writing demonstrates effective skills in responding to the writing benchmark tasks. All traits of quality writing are obvious.

Anchor Charts—Anchor charts are used to track student thinking. In this resource, anchor charts are created cooperatively by the teacher and students. The charts are used to scaffold learning and chart key concepts of writing such as ideas for writing, vocabulary words, and examples of sentence structure. Anchor charts are displayed throughout the room to support a print-rich environment that promotes literacy acquisition.

Anecdotal Observations—Throughout Writer's Workshop, teachers practice the art of becoming astute observers of student writing behaviors. The teacher's Conferring Notebook is an excellent resource to store observations for the entire year of instruction (See Appendix A). As you observe, remember to present a statement of praise and develop a teaching point as this will guide future instructional decisions.

Author's Chair—Students are selected to share their writing with classmates. Usually students sit in a designated chair/stool. Classmates provide feedback to authors in the form of a question or a compliment.

Author's Tea/Author's Luncheon—An author's tea can be held anytime to support student writing efforts. Students invite parents and special loved ones to join them, sometimes with refreshments, to celebrate accomplishments in writing. Each student writes, illustrates, publishes, and presents a favorite piece of writing from the past year. It is important that every student has someone to listen to his or her especially planned presentation. You might invite the principal, cafeteria cook, librarian, or teacher specialists as part of the celebration.

Benchmark Assessments—The beginning-of-the-year benchmark serves as baseline information about a student's writing. Middle-of-the-year and end-of-the-year benchmarks represent a student's progress toward state, district, and/or school benchmark goals.

Terminology Used *(cont.)*

Heads-up, Stand-up, Partner-up—This is an activity in which the teacher gains students' attention, they stand up and quickly move to find partners, and they begin a discussion of focused writing talk. Partners can be assigned based upon the needs of the class or they can be chosen spontaneously. However, it is crucial that students move quickly and in an orderly fashion without any wasted time.

Mentor Texts—A mentor text is a book that offers multiple learning opportunities as both teacher and student develop writing skills. Mentor texts contain explicit and strong examples of the author's craft and are visited repeatedly to explore the traits of quality writing. Your favorite books to share often make the best mentor texts. You may wish to use the recommended mentor text as a read-aloud during your reading block with spirited discussions or quickly review it during Writer's Workshop. During writing block, focus on small samples of text that match the mini-lesson skill. A recommended list of mentor texts is provided as part of each lesson and additional titles are provided in Appendix C.

My Turn/Your Turn—*My Turn* indicates an individual teacher response with students not participating, but watching and listening. *Your Turn* indicates a whole-class group response with everyone participating. Use of hand gestures, with the hand sweeping across the group, palms up is an excellent signal to alert students to respond as a whole group. Recent research has shown that whole group responses eliminate poor behavior decisions, increase motivation, and improve participation. This management strategy is especially helpful for targeting specific writing strategies or having students respond to targeted concepts.

Pinch and Roll—This term refers to a strategy for the proper way to grip a pencil. Students hold their pencils in many positions that produce unnecessary stress on the body. Proper pencil grip requires a three-finger grip, with a roll of the pencil back into the space between the thumb and pointer finger. This is a relaxed, natural way to grip the pencil and eliminates undue writing fatigue.

Turn and Talk—*Turn and Talk* is a management tool for giving opportunities to students to have partner conversations. This procedure may take place at the meeting area or at desks. Students make eye contact, lean toward their partner, talk quietly, or listen attentively.

Triads and Quads—These are terms used to quickly divide the class into groups of three or four.

References

Anderson, Carl. 2000. *How's It Going? A Practical Guide to Conferring with Student Writers*. Portsmouth, NH: Heinemann.

Angelillo, Janet. 2005. *Writing to the Prompt: When Students Don't Have a Choice*. Portsmouth, NH: Heinemann.

Calkins, Lucy M. 1994. *The Art of Teaching Writing* (New ed.). Portsmouth, NH: Heinemann.

Calkins, Lucy M., Amanda Hartman, and Zoe White. 2003. *The Conferring Handbook*. Portsmouth, NH: Heinemann

———. 2005. *One to One: The Art of Conferring with Young Writers*. Portsmouth, NH: Heinemann.

Clay, Marie M. 1975. *What Did I Write?: Beginning Writing Behaviour*. Portsmouth, NH: Heinemann.

Culham, Ruth. 2003. *6 + 1 Traits of Writing: The Complete Guide (Grades 3 and Up)*. New York: Scholastic.

———. 2008. *6 + 1 Traits of Writing: The Complete Guide for the Primary Grades*. New York: Scholastic.

———. 2008. *Using Picture Books to Teach Writing with the Traits K–2*. New York: Scholastic.

Davis, Judy, and Sharon Hill. 2003. *The No-Nonsense Guide to Teaching Writing: Strategies, Structures, Solutions*. Portsmouth, NH: Heinemann.

Dolch, Edward W. 1941. *Teaching Primary Reading*. Champaign, IL: The Garrard Press.

Dorn, Linda J., and Carla Soffos. 2001. *Scaffolding Young Writers: A Writers' Workshop Approach*. Portland, ME: Stenhouse Publishers.

Ehri, Linnea C. 1997. "Learning to Read and Write Are One and the Same, Almost." in *Learning to Spell: Research, Theory, and Practice Across Languages*. Edited by Charles A. Perfetti, Laurence Rieben, and Michael F. Maywah. London: Lawrence Erlbaum Associates.

Elkonin, Daniel B. 1973 *U.S.S.R. in Comparative reading; cross-national studies of behavior and process in reading and writing*. Edited by John A. Downing. New York: Macmillan.

Fletcher, Ralph, and JoAnn Portalupi. 1998. *Craft Lessons: Teaching Writing K–8*. Portland, ME: Stenhouse Publishers.

———. 2001. *Writing Workshop: The Essential Guide*. Portsmouth, NH: Heinemann.

Frayer, Dorothy, Wayne Frederick, and Herbert Klausmeier. 1969. *A Schema for Testing the Level of Cognitive Mastery*. Madison, WI: Wisconsin Center for Education Research.

Freeman, Marcia. 2001. *Non-Fiction Writing Strategies: Using Science Big Books as Models*. Gainesville, FL: Maupin House Publising, Inc.

References (cont.)

———. 1998. *Teaching the Youngest Writers: A Practical Guide.* Gainesville, FL: Maupin House Publishing, Inc.

Gentry, J. Richard. 2000. *The Literacy Map: Guiding Children to Where They Need to Be (K–3).* New York: Mondo Publishing.

———. 2002. *The Literacy Map: Guiding Children to Where They Need to Be (4–6).* New York: Mondo Publishing.

———. 2004. *The Science of Spelling: The Explicit Specifics That Make Greater Readers and Writers (and Spellers!).* Portsmouth, NH: Heinemann

———. 2006. *Breaking the Code: New Science of Beginning Reading and Writing.* Portsmouth, NH: Heinemann.

———. 2007. *Breakthrough in Beginning Reading and Writing.* New York: Scholastic, Inc.

———. 2008. *Step-by-Step: Assessment Guide to Code Breaking.* New York: Scholastic, Inc.

———. 2010. *Raising Confident Readers: How to Teach Your Child to Read and Write—from Baby to Age 7.* Cambridge, MA: Da Capo Lifelong Books.

Gentry, J. Richard., and Jean Gillet. 1993. *Teaching Kids to Spell.* Portsmouth, NH: Heinemann.

Gibson, Vicki. 2004. *We Can! I Can Draw Pre-Writing Program.* Longmont, CO: Sorpris West Educational Services.

Gould, Judith. 1999. *Four Square Writing Method: A Unique Approach to Teaching Basic Writing Skills for Grades 1–3.* Carthage, IL: Teaching and Learning Company.

Graham, Steve, and Michael Hebert. 2010. *Writing to Read: Evidence for How Writing Can Improve Reading. A Carnegie Corporation Time to Act Report.* Washington, DC: Alliance for Excellent Education.

Graves, Donald H. 1994. *A Fresh Look at Writing.* Portsmouth, NH: Heinemann.

———. 2003. *Writing: Teachers and Children at Work 20th Anniversary Edition.* Portsmouth, NH: Heinemann.

Hirsch, Eric, and John Holdren. 1996. *What Your Kindergartner Needs to Know: Preparing Your Child for a Lifetime of Learning.* New York: Dell Publishing.

Jensen, Eric. 2009. *Different Brains, Different Learners: How to Reach the Hard to Reach* (Second ed.). Thousand Oaks, CA: Corwin Press.

Johnston, Peter H. 2004. *Choice Words.* Portland, OR: Stenhouse Publishers.

Koehler, Susan. 2007. *Crafting Expository Papers.* Gainesville, FL: Maupin House Publishing, Inc.

McMahon, Carolyn, and Peggy Warrick. 2005. *We Can Write: Using 6 + 1 Trait Writing Strategies with Renowned Children's Literature.* Portland, OR: Northwest Regional Educational Laboratory.

References (cont.)

Murray, David. 1984. *Write to Learn*. New York: Holt.

National Governors Association Center for Best Practices and Council of Chief State School Officers. 2011. *Common Core State Standards Initiative*: The Standards. Retrieved June 2011, from Common Core State Standards Initiative: http://www.corestandards.org.

Olness, Rebecca. 2004. *Using Literature to Enhance Writing Instruction*. Newark, DE: International Reading Association.

Pearson, David, and Margaret Gallagher. 1983. "The instruction of reading comprehension." *Contemporary Educational Psychology*, 8, 317-344.

Ray, Katie W. 2001. *The Writing Workshop: Working Through the Hard Parts (And They're All Hard Parts)*. Urbana, IL: National Council of Teachers of English.

Ray, Katie W., and Lisa Cleaveland. 2004. *About the Authors: Writing Workshop with Our Youngest Writers*. Portsmouth, NH: Heinemann.

Routman, Regie. 1999. *Conversations: Strategies for Teaching, Learning and Evaluating*. Portsmouth, NH: Heinemann.

———. 2005. *Writing Essentials: Raising Expectations and Results While Simplifying Teaching*. Portsmouth, NH: Heinemann.

Spandel, Vicki. 2001. *Books, Lessons, Ideas for Teaching the Six Traits*. Wilmington, MA: Great Source Education Group.

———. 2005. *Seeing with New Eyes: A Guidebook on Teaching and Assessing Beginning Writers Using the Six-Trait Writing Model* (6th Edition.) Portland, OR: Northwest Regional Educational Laboratory.

———. 2008. *Creating Young Writers: Using the Six Traits to Enrich Writing Process in Primary Classrooms* (2nd Edition ed.) New York: Allyn & Bacon.

Sprenger, Marilee B. 2007. *Becoming a "Wiz" at Brain-Based Teaching: How to Make Every Year Your Best Year*. Thousand Oaks, CA: Corwin Press.

Tate, Marcia. L. 2004. *"Sit and Get" Won't Grow Dendrites*. Thousand Oaks, CA: Corwin Press.

Vygotsky, Lev. 1978. *Mind in Society: The Development of Higher Psychological Processes*. Edited by Michael Cole, Vera John-Steiner, Sylvia Scribner, and Ellen Souberman. Cambridge, MA: Harvard University Press.

Contents of the Teacher Resource CD

Teacher Resources

Page Number	Title	Filename
N/A	Traits Team	traitsteam.pdf
N/A	Student Writing Samples	samples.doc
N/A	Year at a Glance	yearataglance.pdf
12–13	Suggested Pacing Guide	pacingguide.pdf
22–26	Correlation to Standards	standards.pdf
247	Conferring Notebook Cover	cover.pdf
248	Mini-Lesson Log	minilessonlog.pdf
249	Conference Log	conferencelog.pdf
250	Conference Countdown	conferencecountdown.pdf
256	First Grade Writing Rubric	firstgradewritingrubric.pdf
257	First Grade Writing Report	firstgradewritingreport.pdf
258	First Grade Writing Grouping Mat	firstgradegroupingmat.pdf
262–269	Mentor Text List	mentortextlist.pdf
272–274	Writing Paper	writingpaper.pdf

Managing Writer's Workshop

Page Number	Title	Filename
33	Sample Classroom Names Anchor Chart	samplenameschart.pdf
34	Classroom Names	classroomnames.pdf
37	Sample Looks Like, Sounds Like, Feels Like Anchor Chart	lookssoundsfeelschart.pdf
40	Guidelines for Writer's Workshop	guidelineswritersws.pdf
45	Sample Partner Conversation Chart	partnerconversation.pdf
50	I Like/I Wonder Cards	likewondercards.pdf

Print Concepts

Page Number	Title	Filename
59–60	Making Letters	makingletters.pdf

Contents of the Teacher Resource CD *(cont.)*

Ideas

Page Number	Title	Filename
64	Ida, Idea Creator	ida.pdf
69	Idea Bank Cards	ideabankcards.pdf
76	My Expert List	myexpertlist.pdf
79	Places I Love	placesilove.pdf
82	People I Love	peopleilove.pdf

Sentence Fluency

Page Number	Title	Filename
84	Simon, Sentence Builder	simon.pdf
87	Sample Sentence Stems	samplesentencestems.pdf
92	Sentence Builders	sentencebuilders.pdf
95–100	Subject Cards	subjectcards.pdf
103–109	Predicate Cards	predicatecards.pdf
114	Crawlin' Preposition Phrases	crawlinprepphrases.pdf
115	Prepositions	prepositions.pdf
118–121	Sentence Picture Cards	sentencepicturecards.pdf
126	Writing Detective Cards	writingdetectivecards.pdf
127	Be a Writing Detective	bewritingdetective.pdf

Organization

Page Number	Title	Filename
130	Owen, Organization Conductor	owen.pdf
133	My Picture Checklist	picchecklist.pdf
N/A	My Alphabet Book	abcbook.pdf
140	Hand Plan Sample	handplansample.pdf
141	My Hand Plan	myhandplan.pdf
142	Topic Ideas	topicideas.pdf
147	Sample Narratives	samplenarratives.pdf
152	My Friendly Letter	myfriendlyletter.pdf
157	How-to Planner	howtoplanner.pdf
162	5 Ws Poem Planner	5wspoemplanner.pdf

Contents of the Teacher Resource CD *(cont.)*

Word Choice

Page Number	Title	Filename
164	Wally, Word Choice Detective	wally.pdf
167	Learn a Word Chart	learnwordchart.pdf
168	High Frequency Word List	highfreqwordlist.pdf
171	Color Words	colorwords.pdf
172	Number Words	numberwords.pdf
175	Size Words	sizewords.pdf
178	Five Senses Words	fivesenseswords.pdf
179	Say It with Senses!	sayitwithsenses.pdf
180–181	Senses Picture Cards	sensespicturecards.pdf
186	Sample Action Words Anchor Chart	actionanchorchart.pdf
189	My Amazing Words	myamazingwords.pdf
192	Transition Words Cards	transitionwordscards.pdf
193–194	Sequencing Picture Cards	sequencingcards.pdf
197–202	Onomatopoeia Dictionary	onomatopoeiadic.pdf
203–204	Teacher Resources for Onomatopoeia	teacheronomatopoeia.pdf

Voice

Page Number	Title	Filename
206	Val and Van Voice	valvan.pdf
209	My Feelings	myfeelings.pdf

Contents of the Teacher Resource CD *(cont.)*

Conventions

Page Number	Title	Filename
214	Callie, Super Conventions Checker	callie.pdf
217	Alphabet Chart	alphabetchart.pdf
220	Capital Rap	capitalrap.pdf
223–224	Vowel Chart	vowelchart.pdf
225	Vowel Word List	vowelwordlist.pdf
228	Hear It! Say It! Sound Boxes	hearsaysoundboxes.pdf
229	Hear It! Say It! Sound Box Word List	hearsaysoundwordlist.pdf
232	Movin' to Edit	movintoedit.pdf
235–236	Digraphs and Consonant Blends Sound Chart	blendschart.pdf
239	My Writing Checklist	mywritingchecklist.pdf
242	Perfect Punctuation Chart	punctuationchart.pdf
245	My Editing Guide	myeditingguide.pdf

Notes

Notes